10th Teaching Innovation & Entrepreneurship Excellence Awards 2024

An Anthology of Case Histories

Edited by Dan Remenyi

Copyright © 2024 The authors

First published September 2024

All rights reserved. Except for the quotation of short passages for the purposes of critical review, no part of this publication may be reproduced in any material form (including photocopying or storing in any medium by electronic means and whether or not transiently or incidentally to some other use of this publication) without the written permission of the copyright holder except in accordance with the provisions of the Copyright Designs and Patents Act 1988, or under the terms of a licence issued by the Copyright Licensing Agency Ltd, Saffron House, 6-10 Kirby Street, London EC1N 8TS. Applications for the copyright holder's written permission to reproduce any part of this publication should be addressed to the publishers.

Disclaimer: While every effort has been made by the editor, authors and the publishers to ensure that all the material in this book is accurate and correct at the time of going to press, any error made by readers as a result of any of the material, formulae or other information in this book is the sole responsibility of the reader. Readers should be aware that the URLs quoted in the book may change or be damaged by malware between the time of publishing and accessing by readers.

Note to readers: Some papers have been written by authors who use the American form of spelling and some use the British. These two different approaches have been left unchanged.

ISBN 978-1-917204-12-5

Published by: Academic Conferences International, Reading, United Kingdom, info@academic-conferences.org

Available from www.academic-bookshop.com

Contents

A Complex Innovation Process: Experiential and Playful Learning (REALGAME)
Milton F. Barragán-Landy 1

Enhancing Active Learning and Industry-Oriented Teaching Design through Competency-Based Education (CBE) Approach: The Case of Start-up Lab Course at HCT- AL Ain Campuses.
Anji Benhamed 19

Entrepreneurship and Innovation: Be inspired
Gaël Bertrand 31

Connecting Dots: Enhancing Students' Research Skills by Developing Sustainability-oriented Entrepreneurial Projects
Gyuzel Gadelshina and Nikolaos Goumagias 47

Fostering Innovation Through Integration:The Bath Entrepreneurship Programme's Comprehensive Approach.
Pascal Loizeau 59

Empowering Change: The Crowdfunding Learning Experience in Entrepreneurial Education
Daniel Michelis 75

Educating for Innovation – And on how Negative Responses to Innovation Abound
Manuel Au-Yong-Oliveira 87

Democratizing Entrepreneurship and Innovation Education Through "No-Code" AI Platforms
Leif Sundberg and Jonny Holmström 101

Acknowledgements

We would like to thank the judges, who initially read the abstracts of the case histories submitted to the competition and discussed these to select those to be submitted as full case histories. These judges will listen to the finalists present their cases at the European Conferences on Innovation and Entrepreneurship at CESI, Paris-Nanterre, France and will select the winner. We would also like to thank the team of reviewers who performed a double-blind review of the entries and made further selections to produce the finalists who are published in this book.

Dr Christopher Moon FRSA FHEA is a multi-award winning social and eco-entrepreneur with a PhD from Imperial College London. He is the founder of several eco-businesses including eco-design-and-build, eco-taxis and buy-eco. Chris is also inspiring business students at Middlesex University London to be more environmentally friendly. He is widely published including a book for the Economist; and is the inventor developer of the award winning patented eco-bin. Chris was a finalist in the Innovation & Entrepreneurship Teaching Excellence Awards 2015. He is a psychologist by background; certified and accredited CSR consultant and Social Auditor.

Dr Ken Grant is a professor of entrepreneurship and strategy in the Ted Rogers School of Business Management He is a visiting professor in the UK, Europe and Asia. His research interests include strategy, entrepreneurship, knowledge management and innovation, and pedagogy. He is an active coach and supporter of student entrepreneur activity across the university and is currently working to facilitate the development of entrepreneurship programs in China. Prior to joining Ryerson, Dr. Grant had an extensive career as a management consultant and industry executive in Canada and the UK, leading global consulting practices in several major firms. He holds a BA degree from the Open University, an MBA from the Schulich School of Business and a DBA from Henley Business School.

Christy Suciu completed her graduate degree at Webster University and teaches in the College of Business and Economics at Boise State University in the area of design thinking, innovation, and strategy. She has created all three design thinking and strategy courses in the different M.B.A. programs. Over the years she has served as a design thinking consultant for many major companies such as HP, Wells Fargo, Paksense, and Biomark. Her research has been published in the Academy of Management Learning and Education and titled, "The need for Design Thinking in Business Schools".

Introduction

Innovation and entrepreneurship skills are more crucial today than ever, both for individuals embarking on new business ventures and for employers seeking to foster these abilities within their teams. However, teaching and learning these skills have always presented challenges. Some universities offer dedicated degrees or courses in these areas, while others integrate these topics across various programs. Regardless of the approach, teaching innovation and entrepreneurship remains difficult, as does conducting research in these fields. The courses and modules are often heavily theoretical and may not provide the practical skills needed, nor effectively inspire students to become innovators or entrepreneurs. Nevertheless, promising work is being done globally to address these challenges, and this annual competition aims to showcase such efforts.

This year, the 10th Teaching Innovation and Entrepreneurship Excellence Awards reflects the innovative practices implemented worldwide. Out of 21 initial submissions, 12 participants were invited to provide a full case history detailing their initiatives. The case histories covered a wide range of topics, making it a challenging task for the review panel to select the most compelling, creative, and innovative entries for the final shortlist published in this anthology. Eight authors or teams were invited to present their work at the European Conference on Innovation and Entrepreneurship, supported by CESI, Paris-Nanterre University in France. The specific topics covered by these presentations can be found on the Contents page of this book.

I extend my gratitude to all contributors for their outstanding efforts in developing new and engaging methods for teaching Innovation and Entrepreneurship. I also want to thank the panel of reviewers and expert judges for their invaluable contributions.

Dan Remenyi PhD
Editor
September 2024

A Complex Innovation Process: Experiential and Playful Learning (REALGAME)

Milton F. Barragán-Landy
Department of Applied Chemistry and Production Systems, Faculty of Chemical Sciences, University of Cuenca, Cuenca – Ecuador
https://orcid.org/0000-0003-4623-6150
mfrancisco.barraganl@ucuenca.edu.ec

Abstract: Teaching innovation is a perennial evolving strategy within the teaching-learning process. It seeks to provide an enriching experience of intangible value to future professionals. In the innovation management chair, it is no exception because it is required to generate innovation processes to teach innovation. The development of recreational games could cause creativity to flow and, above all, experiential learning processes give students greater interest in learning. This is justified because students seek greater pragmatism or more practical tools. This proposal tries to analyse the introduction of endogenous and exogenous learning development processes at the same time so that, from their personal creativity, their learning can be improved. The proposal is called Real Game. The methodology has four phases: (i) introduction of concepts; (ii) execution of the practice; (iii) analysis of results and feedback; and (iv) learning achieved. This process was carried out in 2 groups of students who were a total of 19. They were then evaluated at the end with problem-solving projects to measure their level of creativity and the application of innovation management techniques. Lego serious play, materials construction and experiential visits to different organizational spaces were used. The great challenge was to break paradigms and stereotypes of class development in the traditional classroom.

1. Introduction

Innovation is a strategy in constant evolution within the teaching-learning process. The aim is to provide an enriching experience of intangible value to future Industrial Engineering professionals. This proposal was developed in Cuenca city in the south of Ecuador country. On the one hand, seeking new participation mechanisms leads to generating new ways of doing things; On the other hand, seeking to generate disruptive processes in order to achieve different results. Thus, interacting and generating greater value to the professional training process could improve the firms' innovation processes. However, the professionals need to improve skills dynamic to respond to the turbulent environments (Mack, O., Khare, A., Kramer, A., & Burgartz, 2015; Millar et al., 2018).

Service Innovation (SI) is a topic of great interest today due to the great intangible value through a logic of service vision (Verma & Rajagopal, 2013). SI is a type of innovation which challenges firms to reduce the gap or distance between them and their customers (Rew et al., 2018). It could contribute towards servitization processes (Zhang & Banerji, 2017) because when the environment constantly changes, it is necessary to strengthen the soft skills of professionals so that their professional actions are more dynamic and adaptive. That is, this proposal seeks to change the traditional practice in the learning – teaching process in the context of Cuenca.

In the innovation management subject is required to generate innovation processes to teach innovation. Thus, this proposal contributes to show an alternative and emerge ludic activity. This strengthens the theory of learning behaviourism. However, the development of recreational games could make creativity flow and, above all, experiential learning processes give students a greater interest in learning (Rodríguez-Jiménez et al., 2022). Also, greater motivation from a participant. This is justified because students seek greater pragmatism or more practical tools in the development of their daily, personal and professional activities. REALGAME try to integrate ludic, experiential and technic aspects. This proposal attempts to analyse the introduction of endogenous and exogenous learning development processes at the same time so that, from your personal creativity, you can improve your learning.

The most important role currently in the teaching - learning process is to be able to offer a different alternative to the technological boom that, although it is the current reality and is growing rapidly; it not necessary to eliminated; but rather to integrated it. This could be a complex and challenges for the future. Some characteristics or factors that this proposal facilitates are the interaction between people on a permanent basis; dialectics, active participation; empowerment, critical reflection, the development of socio-emotional skills and, above all, flexibility processes. They could help strengthen a process of emancipatory education. This with the objective that students acquire a meaning so that it is integrated into their existing cognitive structure.

The aim of this proposal seeks to provide an enriching experience of intangible value to future industrial engineering professionals. This was done in connection with the participants' stimulation to prove new methods for the learning process in the innovation management subject.

2. The infrastructure

The method is called REALGAME. The methodology used is based on respecting the learning achievements that are planned at the beginning of the development of the Innovation Management subject, then during the development of the classes the technique is perfected considering the attitude and aptitude of the group of students.

It is important to note which to establish a prior adaptation process according to the established methodology is necessary. That is, the teacher must prepare students for this process though some initial considerations (Achig Subía, 2011):

- to develop predisposition to learn; that is, the understanding of the student to leverage some of its learning.
- the material used must have a logical structure and the game must be classified as something serious and funny at the same time.
- to develop of learning capabilities that allow them to interact with the new learning proposal through previous interactions.
- The concepts should flow in a structured and hierarchical way to be able to develop them in the development of their learning.
- The game process establishes that any critical opinion or question is important. Within this process, the students' emotions are visualized by being able to express your ideas with the created representation and the concepts developed.
- The game establishes emotional processes that stimulate the integration of learning from an endogenous perspective.

It is expected when applying this complex methodology which integrates; theoretical concepts, realities of the environment, game, emotions and others when executing the process can develop some skills among its practitioners (Achig Subía, 2011): (i) openness to learning, this because being a game the students are motivated to be able to investigate more about the concepts and want continue building their learning with play; In addition to being a mechanism to break the fear of speaking and various other feelings they experience; (ii) behaviour change, aimed at always seeking to improve and seeing reality from a game to be able to interpret, relate, and reflect on the use of this process; (iii) discovery and understanding, being a disruptive methodology in the context where it is applied, generates concern, curiosity and, above all, openness to try and experience it.

Figure 1 presents the phases of this proposal.

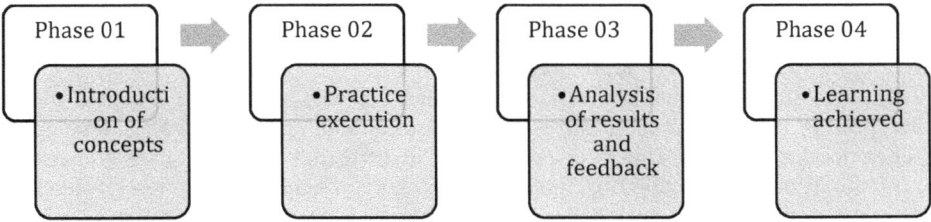

Figure 1. RealGame Phases.

Introduction of concepts

This section introduces participants to the key concepts within the development of the innovation management subject. The concepts are presented from two approaches: (i) through the concrete reading of concepts in books and papers; and (ii) through the game the concept of what is intended to be established is established. That is, the concepts are introduced before, during or after the execution of the game with its dynamics. The concepts are co-created at the same time and/or the concepts are developed.

Execution of the practice

An objective of the practice is established, which is related to a specific concept; Subsequently, students begin to develop their idea through its interpretation in the game of Lego blocks or with recycled material (tubes) where they seek to build a specific object (Figure 2). It is important to note that while the process of assembling the pieces was carried out, different types of environments conditions adapted were used. Instrumental music that established the class work rhythm. Thus, a slow sound is used to reflect and a loud sound and fast musical notes to accelerate the concentration process during the assembling.

Figure 2. Creating knowledge.

Analysis of results and feedback

The most important and imperative is the use of "analogies" as a mechanism for interpreting the concept and, above all, for understanding what is being developed. When building a figure. This can be interpreted in different ways and is the key; because perceptions are diverse and multiple and learning approaches can be more in-depth in their development. The only one who interprets it is the student from his individual perception and by showing it and dialoguing with his classmates, learning is built because it is fed back by all those who listen to the interpretation. The teacher seeks to understand the developed concept or the established integration of concepts from the interpretation of each student and later give feedback too.

Learning achieved

The results achieved are systematized in a report, which presents the schematization of the ideas and, above all, conclusions and reflections that were reached when developing the work. Also, the concepts integration to respond to the students' questions

Note: Four examples of participant reports are available in the appendix. They were executed in a class established to learn a specific concept; that was translated to the English language.

3. The challenges

This process was carried out in 2 groups of students that were a total of 19. During their training process, their performance and, above all, their learning was evaluated, which was structured from several aspects. They were then evaluated at the end with problem-solving projects to measure their level of creativity and application of innovation management techniques. The great challenge was to break paradigms and stereotypes of class development in the traditional classroom. The change in behaviour, motivation and attitude in participants is a reality that is reflected when using this mixed technique.

The first group of students participated in the process in 2022 and are currently working as Industrial Engineers and the second group is in the graduation process this year 2024. Information was collected through an expanded semi-structured survey to find out their current situation (Saunders et al., 2016). The data reflects major challenges that were grouped by categories for a better understanding. Table 1 shows the challenges and comments of the participants

Table 1. Challenges and Participants Comments

Challenges	Participants Comments
Creativity in the object generation	"Being abstract it becomes difficult to execute the activity" "To portray the situations requested by the lecturer with Lego pieces" "Initial block to develop new solutions and designs" "Work with other people, with creative differences, reach consensus and share ideas"
Adaptation of the method	"A new approach to work" "I have not used blocks and in this activity I do it to learn by playing"
Time management	"Time to think about the idea of structure"
Large work groups	"almost impossible to hear all the opinions of the participants and the limitations of the material"
Communication and coordination	"some tasks require communicating clearly with your classmates"
Set leader	"As we are trained to be leaders, it is difficult to assign who the leader is"

In addition, the students were asked on a Likert scale; whether they experienced any difficulty in initially adapting to the playful approach of the game compared to traditional teaching methods.

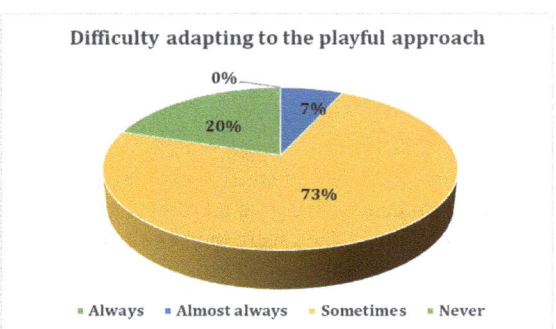

Figure 3. Difficulty adapting to the playful approach

Figure 3 shows the results. 73% of those surveyed stated "sometimes" that they had difficulty; This makes sense when implementing a new paradigm in the teaching-learning process. Followed by 20% who mention that they "never" had difficulty; 7% indicate that "almost always" the interactions presented some type of difficulty and finally 0% in the "always" option. These results denote a dynamic process and emotions that students have.

4. How the initiative was received

In relation with the initiative how was received by the users or participants; a survey was made to respond it. A survey was established in the 2 working groups to provide feedback on the work proposal. Table 2 presents the principal participant comments to understand from their position categorized by aspect.

Table 2. Participants perceptions by aspect

Aspects	Participants perceptions
Understanding of concepts	"The development of these activities allowed us to better understand the concepts seen, the development of sensory skills"
	"Experience a new way of understanding a topic"
	"They are very dynamic activities that unconsciously teach the main concepts of the topic, which are usually reviewed before or after"
	"Based on what has been experienced in the classroom, it is interesting to apply recreational activities because we can better experience the theory presented in class, in cases that can be compared with reality"

Aspects	Participants perceptions
Critical thinking	"They were very innovative exercises, which allowed the development of critical thinking through playful learning"
	"It allowed the development of creativity, in addition to identifying what the participant's strength was"
Emerging method	Playful activities are presented as an alternative to conventional teaching methods, which aim to address teaching criteria from a perspective that appeals much more to the student's creativity.
	The recreational activities have had clear objectives and purposes, they are interactive and allow us to learn in an innovative way since clear instructions are provided and constructive feedback is provided on the specific topic.
Holistic Thinking	"Very grateful for the idea of generating knowledge in a different way. I can say that I not only learned the knowledge of Lean Service and Innovation Management but lived it".
	"They are activities full of learning in a different way, their application is highly recommended and in one way or another they allow the student to expand their capacity to develop theoretical concepts".

In addition, the participants were asked how the experimental and playful game facilitated their understanding and application of concepts in the subject. Figure 4 shows the results. 80% of respondents indicate the category "Strongly"; That is to say, they understand the concepts better and can interpret them equally; 13% think "Moderately", 7% "Little" and finally 0% "nil" about the application process. The results show to be mostly favorable the proposal methodology.

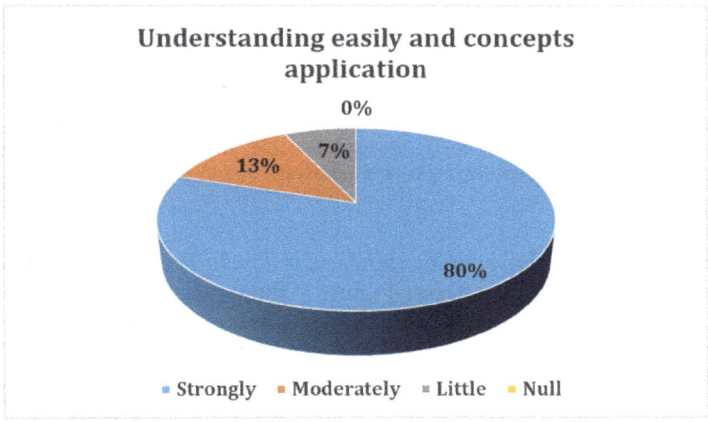

Figure 4. Understanding easily and concepts application

5. The learning outcomes

The objective of the Innovation Management subject allows the student to learn about the innovation process, the different types and intervention strategies in organizations that provide services. Furthermore, the subject aims to describe the relationship between creativity and innovation within the framework of the development of innovative and sustainable services. Table 3 shows the skills developed and their description.

The learning achievements were established based on what was planned in the subject and were the following:

- To analyse different scenarios of business life and articulate them with innovation.
- To describe the relationship between creativity and innovation within the framework of the development of innovative products.
- To analyse techniques to develop innovation skills with the market.
- To identify innovation strategies in services.

Table 3. Skills description in relation with the learning outcomes

Skills	Description
Teamwork	-Teamwork, communication, problem solving, adaptability, time management, leadership, innovation and above all creativity. -Teamwork, communication, time management (working under pressure), adaptability, flexibility and problem solving.
Critical Thinking	- To work under pressure. Resolution of problems. -Ability to represent ideas in physical material (Legos), rather than simply verbalizing ideas. -Be able to share and compare ideas about the same concept with different colleagues and discuss it.
Understanding innovation	Experiencing the feeling of being present in the problem, understanding it first deductively and then inductively by having a "layman" physical anchor to organize the ideas.
Adaptability	Consider that in games you necessarily try to adapt what the lecturer asked for to a specific topic, therefore, in one way or another adaptability is strengthened.

In relation with the playful activity satisfaction level. The students indicated their perception of the developed process. Figure 5 shows the results. 67% indicate the category of "Very satisfied" and 33% "Satisfied", indicating that there is a favourable perception of the job proposal presented; However, like everything, it can be perfected. This requires critical thinking for be able to move forward in the process of continuous improvement.

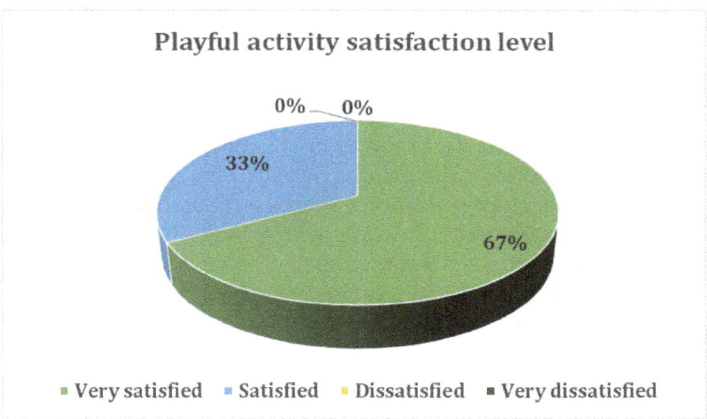

Figure 5. Playful activity satisfaction level

6. Plans to further develop the initiative

The methodology presents some opportunities for continuous improvement that are framed in strengthening the interaction of the participants and, above all, value their learning. In the same way, their main needs were identified through a semi-structured survey:

The main plan for the future for improvement are framed in:

- To adapt new tools that complement the activities, for example simulators that represent the topic or project creation.
- To record the data results of the proposal execution process in an improved manner.
- To improve the time established for the execution of exercises through projects with Industry cases; identified from their pre-professional practice or their actions in companies. Solve playful exercises with implicit and collaborative learning.
- To increase the level of complexity with a high level of pressure as possible to be able to respond to a potential reality.
- To actively listen to participants about the opinions they have regarding these dynamics in order to establish feedback processes.
- To motivate and increase the desire to learn and actively participate; through extra points for their actions.
- To include the use of technology for recreational activities such as simulators in processes of Industrial Engineering.
- To develop digital guides or a physical version of the executed process; or through videos continue including the reflection of each activity.

- To diversify the use of new Lego pieces for the development of more activities.

7. Conclusion and Reflection

The objective of the proposal is to generate innovation processes in order to teach innovation. That is to say, seeking a process of coherence between what is taught and what is experienced in the classroom. Lego Serious play, materials construction and experiential visits to different organizational spaces were used. The great challenge was to break paradigms and stereotypes of class development in the classroom. This is in relation to incorporate disruptive methods in the context of Cuenca, Ecuador. The change in behaviour, motivation and attitude in students is a reality that is reflected when using this mixed technique. Likewise, several complementary reading books were used through flipped classroom presented by the students with the same REALGAME. Other application was the critical thinking incorporation during of the sessions. This helped to improve the proposal before, during and after of the implementation.

References

Achig Subía, L. (2011). Aprendizajes en la educación.

Mack, O., Khare, A., Kramer, A., & Burgartz, T. (Eds. . (2015). Managing in a VUCA World. Springer.

Millar, C. C. J. M., Groth, O., & Mahon, J. F. (2018). Management Innovation in a VUCA World: Challenges and Recommendations. California Management Review, 61(1), 5–14. https://doi.org/10.1177/0008125618805111

Rew, D., Jung, J., & Cha, W. (2018). Service productivity vs service quality: a zero-sum game? International Journal of Quality & Reliability Management, 35(9), 1835–1852. https://doi.org/10.1108/IJQRM-01-2017-0019

Rodríguez-Jiménez, O., Garcia-Pinilla, J. I., Pineda, B., Malaver, J. A., & Galindo León, E. A. (2022). Methodi Quantitative: A Ludic Way for Learning Quantitative Methodology in Psychology BT - Mobility for Smart Cities and Regional Development - Challenges for Higher Education (M. E. Auer, H. Hortsch, O. Michler, & T. Köhler (eds.); pp. 119–126). Springer International Publishing.

Saunders, M., Lewis, P., & Thornhill, A. (2016). Research Methods for Business Students (Seventh Ed). Pearson Education Limited.

Verma, R., & Rajagopal. (2013). Conceptualizing Service Innovation Architecture: A Service-Strategic Framework. Journal of Transnational Management, 18(1), 3–22. https://doi.org/10.1080/15475778.2013.751869

Weigel, S., & Hadwich, K. (2018). Success factors of service networks in the context of servitization – Development and verification of an impact model. Industrial Marketing Management, 74, 254–275. https://doi.org/https://doi.org/10.1016/j.indmarman.2018.06.002

Zhang, W., & Banerji, S. (2017). Challenges of servitization: A systematic literature review. Industrial Marketing Management, 65, 217–227. https://doi.org/https://doi.org/10.1016/j.indmarman.2017.06.003

Milton F. Barragán-Landy

Appendix

Participant Report # 1

UNIVERSITY OF CUENCA
FACULTY OF CHEMICAL SCIENCES
INDUSTRIAL ENGINEERING CAREER

Name: Garay Domenica, Velecela Anthony

Practice Report #3: Evolutionary process of technological change and technology of change

Date: May 2nd, 2024

Objective: To analyse the evolution of food consumption

Activity: Bread making

How bread was consumed before	
	In the past, bread was made with rudimentary methods that depended on the resources available. The image represents how the bread dough was placed on a hot stone heated by the sun. Another way was to put the dough directly on or around the fire, where it cooked slowly and it was necessary to make sure that all sides of the dough were cooked bread will be cooked and will not be raw.
How bread is consumed today	
	Currently, breads are made in wood-burning ovens or gas ovens; now you can control the temperature or the amount of fire with the flammable material used. Now we have an idea of how much time should be left for cooking and this remains as a standard measure. A greater number of breads can be made in a single batch than the oven can make. The baker requires skill, as well as experience.

How will bread be consumed in 5 years?	In the next five years, it is likely that ovens will not change much, but the evolution of bread ovens may be more focused on optimizing materials to improve energy and durability, as well as reducing baking times while maintaining the quality of the bread. Loading and unloading of the oven will be facilitated, with tray transportation and rotation systems, which would increase productivity and remove hot loaves every time the oven opens to remove one.
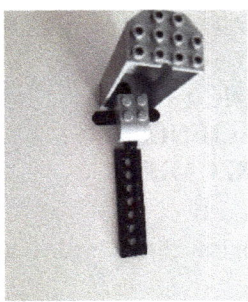	
How will bread be consumed in 10 years?	In the future, machines will appear that change the concept of baking much more, so that the process is even more simplified. This involves allowing humans to simply add ingredients and press a button, turning out fresh, perfectly baked bread without the need for kneading or proofing, which is often the most tedious part of bread making. Functioning similar to a toaster.

How will bread be consumed in 30 years?	In the distant future we will see a radical transformation with the introduction of 3D printing technology. This could allow the creation of personalized breads based on consumer preferences, where not only the type of ingredient (wheat, rye, barley, etc.) can be chosen, but also the dietary composition, such as gluten-free, keto or other options. This revolutionary technology would not only offer a greater diversity of products, but could also promote a more personalized and healthy diet.

- Technological change has a significant impact on human development in many aspects, including the way we relate to the world, how we work, how we communicate and also how we eat. On the other hand, change technology focuses on using technology as a strategic tool to drive and manage specific changes in different areas of human life; However, both approaches are complementary and are aimed at the evolution of technology and its strategic application to promote transformations in society.

- Regarding food and many aspects of our daily lives, these new techniques present exciting opportunities to improve our quality of life, but also important challenges that must be addressed ethically and equitably to ensure positive and sustainable human development. The key is to take advantage of the benefits of technology while mitigating its possible adverse effects, working towards a future in this food case; healthier, inclusive and conscious.

Participant Report # 2
UNIVERSITY OF CUENCA
FACULTY OF CHEMICAL SCIENCES
INDUSTRIAL ENGINEERING CAREER

Name: Siavichay Adrián

Practice Report #2: Disruptions

Objective: To develop a disruptive mean of transportation

Date: April 2nd, 2023

Activity: In this case, we start by representing a conventional means of transportation (car) and then propose a disruptive means of transportation

Activity	Descriptions	Illustration
Automobile representation	The notable attributes of a car are: - Comfort - Availability for several people - Audio quality - Elegant design - Small size - Speed - Loading capacity	
Disruption	For this design, the characteristics of a conventional automobile that are essential for a means of transportation were considered. The new design has the following features: - Modularity (if I add a module I increase the capacity). - It uses a hybrid system of wheels and propellers. Depending on time availability and the destination you can choose which one to use. - It is autonomous.	

The 10th Innovation & Entrepreneurship Teaching Excellence Awards

	- It has an audio and video entertainment system integrated throughout the vehicle. - Comfortable and elegant interior design.	

In this specific case, when analysing the background of the creator, the design result is the set of experiences and desires stored in the conscious or unconscious of the individual. The greater the number of different experiences available, the easier the development of the design will be and with a higher degree of originality. It would be advisable to expose the idea to a group of people in which there are detractors and people in favour, with a high degree of interest and knowledge of the subject, to establish a better criterion of the design and the scope that it will have if it becomes a reality a formal project.

Participant Report # 3

UNIVERSITY OF CUENCA
FACULTY OF CHEMICAL SCIENCES
INDUSTRIAL ENGINEERING CAREER

Name: Siavichay Adrián
Practice Report #8: Disruptive Figure
Objective: To create a disruptive figure based on adaptive attributes that can then be converted into an innovative service.
Date: June 29th, 2023

Activity: For this case, it began by "prescribing the brain" using motor skill techniques with the hands. Then, we proceeded to create an object that can adapt to any surface, giving it unique attributes for said objective. Finally, focus was placed on three attributes that could be improved, with this, a way to create a unique service was devised from the "Disruptive Figure".

Description	Illustration
A complement was created for the human being, through which any space can be accessed, be it soil, water or air. (Initial design)	

Granted Attributes 1. Fly 2. Adapts to desert terrain 3. Fleet 4. Can be mechanically driven by human 5. It has great speed 6. It is comfortable 7. It is for use by one person only 8. It's lightweight 9. It is easy to store 10. It has no fuel limitations Attributes chosen to improve: 1. Fly: Use Aero gliders without electrical or mechanical drive. 2. Adaptable to any type of soil: It uses a wheel that can be driven by an electric motor or mechanically by the user. 3. Fleet: The versatility of the wheel, in addition to adapting to different types of soil, It can serve as a turbine in aquatic environments.	
Innovative Service: Rental of units for sporting events. The objective is to create a new long-distance sport (over 500 km) in which the object is used as a hybrid discipline (Land, air and water). The target audience is lovers of extreme sports. The business model would be focused on two areas, event planning and equipment rental.	

The practice allowed us to explore new options for generating business based on services. By having total freedom at the beginning, it is possible to eliminate previous barriers or paradigms and make way for devising new scenarios. By giving attributes to the object, the problems and needs unconsciously hidden in the creator are reflected and which may be viable as a business model.

Participant Report # 4

UNIVERSITY OF CUENCA
FACULTY OF CHEMICAL SCIENCES
INDUSTRIAL ENGINEERING CAREER

Name: Group work - Project extract
Date: April 04th, 2024

The 10th Innovation & Entrepreneurship Teaching Excellence Awards

Project: The objective is to join 10 PVC pipes (in pairs) 20 cm long and 3 inches in diameter, divided horizontally in half. The bottom part must be complete and its interior should be as smooth as possible. In addition, the upper part must have 2 windows symmetrical. It is important that the final product be disassembled. Finally, it must standardize the process.

Project justification: The project seeks to apply the concept of Quality Route reviewed in class through a practical and collaborative project. Focuses on continuous improvement and finding the method optimal for its execution.

Goal: The goal is to join a pair of PVC pipes with sufficiently precise cuts, ensuring that the piece bottom has an acceptably smooth interior. Furthermore, it is sought that the upper part has two symmetrical windows. The final product must be disassembled and the joining process be standardized to maintain an acceptable level of quality and efficiency.

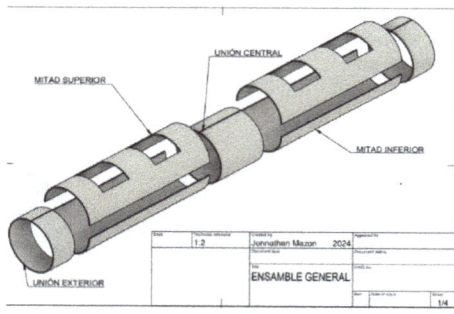

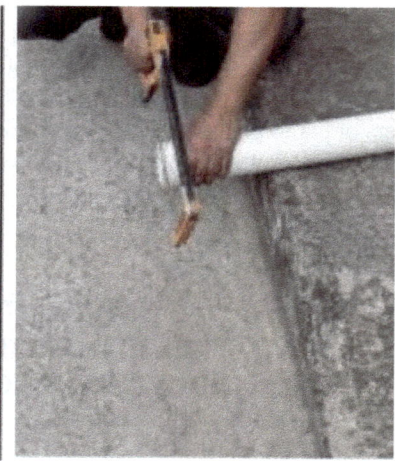

JM: Participating in this project has been an enriching experience. Not only have we learned about teamwork and project management, but we have also applied quality tools that have helped us improve our product. In addition to the technical aspects, we have valued skills such as effective communication, collaboration and problem solving.

DN: Applying the quality route in project execution and promoting teamwork are complementary strategies that have a significant impact on product quality. Additionally, teamwork allows us to identify and address the root causes of quality problems early, resulting in significant operational cost reductions.

JF: In conclusion, adopting a continuous improvement approach has been essential to raising standards of product quality and functionality. By carefully identifying challenges in tube measurements, one that was not meeting our objectives, we opted to restart the process. This decision allowed us to implement more effective solutions and achieve even higher levels of excellence.

Author Biography

Milton F. Barragán-Landy is Lecturer and Researcher from 2010. His research interests are Quality, Innovation and Complexity in the Service Industry; Agile, Resilience and Project Management. He has experience in the sector of goods production included in the sectors of mechanical metal, ceramics and food in the topics of total quality, logistics, health and safety of the human factor. Also in the service sector: human talent management, strategic process and quality management, and director of the Industrial Engineering and Innovation Research Group.

Enhancing Active Learning and Industry-Oriented Teaching Design through Competency-Based Education (CBE) Approach: The Case of Start-up Lab Course at HCT- AL Ain Campuses.

Anji Benhamed
Business faculty, Higher Colleges of technology HCT, UAE
abenhamed@hct.ac.ae
Anjibenhamed@gmail.com

1. Introduction

In the rapidly evolving landscape of education and professional development, Competency-Based Education (CBE) emerges as a transformative approach, especially pertinent for startup courses. Unlike traditional education models that rely on a time-based progression, CBE emphasizes the mastery of specific skills and competencies, ensuring that learners acquire the essential knowledge and abilities required in the dynamic startup ecosystem. This case analysis explores the implementation and impact of CBE in a startup course, examining how this model aligns with the unique demands of entrepreneurial education, fosters practical skill acquisition, and enhances learner engagement and outcomes. Through a detailed examination of real-world applications and outcomes, this analysis aims to provide insights into the effectiveness of CBE in preparing individuals for the challenges and opportunities within the startup sector.

2. Competency-Based Education (CBE) Approach

The literature on Competency-Based Education (CBE) highlights its potential to revolutionize learning by prioritizing skill mastery over traditional time-based education models. According to Guskey and Jung (2013), CBE frameworks are designed to ensure that learners achieve specific competencies before progressing, which can be particularly effective in fields requiring practical and applied skills. Research by Ford (2014) emphasizes the adaptability of CBE in professional and technical education, where tailored learning paths can address individual learner needs and industry demands. In the context of entrepreneurial education, Morris et al. (2015) argue that CBE can foster innovation and critical thinking skills essential for startup ecosystem. Moreover, studies such as those by Klein-Collins (2012) suggest that CBE programs can improve learner engagement and outcomes by providing more relevant and flexible learning experiences. This body of literature underscores the suitability of

CBE for startup lab courses, where the focus is on equipping learners with the competencies required to thrive in fast-paced, innovation-driven settings.

3. The Case of Start-up Lab Course

The Startup Lab course provides an immersive and practical learning experience, guiding students through the entire process of creating and validating innovative business ideas that meet genuine market needs. The curriculum is designed to offer a thorough understanding of startup development methodologies, covering essential stages such as idea generation, comprehensive market research, prototype design, customer acquisition strategies, and business model formulation. The course culminates with students presenting and defending a comprehensive business plan to potential stakeholders and a panel of industry experts. This hands-on approach, aligned with the principles of CBE, ensures that students not only learn theoretical concepts but also apply them in real-world scenarios, thereby bridging the gap between education and practical application in the entrepreneurial field.

To achieve the objectives of the Startup Lab, we have integrated two effective constructionist learning strategies: Project-Based Learning (PBL) and the Competency-Based Education (CBE) model as applied at HCT. This blended approach has proven to be effective in delivering robust educational tools and fostering a dynamic entrepreneurial experience. The goal is to empower students by enhancing their practical entrepreneurial skills and knowledge, aligning their abilities with industry requirements and the startup ecosystem, and helping them clarify their long-term entrepreneurial career goals.

Our competency-based educational model places equal emphasis on theoretical knowledge and practical skills gained through engaging learning activities and immersive experiences with clearly defined outcomes. The Startup Lab's PBL-CBE framework is built on:

- Defining and achieving specific competencies relevant to the startup world.
- Allowing students to progress at their own pace to gain a deeper understanding of startup requirements, challenges, and scope.
- Focusing on the real-world applicability of all concepts related to startups and new venture creation.

The design of this initiative is based on the CBE framework, which is founded on the principle of Social Constructivism. It incorporates the five E pillars model: Engagement, Exploration, Explanation, Elaboration, and Evaluation.

4. The infrastructure

Over the past two years, the Project based approach and the CBE were gradually implemented in the course to create a student-centered learning environment, supported by the necessary infrastructure including activities, exercises, and software such as

Figma, Porto.io. The weekly content delivery has been transformed into mini-workshops, where students actively lead or participate in gaming activities focused on startups and innovation. The instructor's role evolved into that of a facilitator, coach, and mentor, leveraging teaching approaches such as Design Thinking, ideation through Lego serious play, Lean Startups Methodology, Entrepreneurial Gaming, Canvas Model, Storytelling for Pitching, Prototyping, Practical Demonstrations, Group Challenges, and Vlogs.

The integration of entrepreneurial gaming and workshops into the course sessions became fundamental to knowledge sharing. Topics such as idea generation, feasibility analysis, entrepreneurial mindset and skills, and the startup ecosystem were explored through engaging activities. Students were involved in brainstorming sessions, creativity exercises, storyboard and storytelling workshops, self-assessment of entrepreneurial mindset tests, 1-minute pitch competitions, design thinking exercises, social media and marketing campaigns for startups, as well as paper-based and digital prototype design, and field trips.

To further emphasize the practical aspect of the course, students engaged in hands-on activities and projects set in real-world scenarios. The pinnacle of the course experience was the Startup-Lab Demo Day event at HCT-AAC. This event marked the culmination of the course, allowing students to showcase their business concepts, promote their solutions through marketing campaigns, and present their startup prototypes (Minimum Viable Products). The event featured booth exhibitions, pitch sessions, and prototype demonstrations, providing students with real-world exposure and valuable market validation feedback from expert audiences.

As a testament to the course's commitment to bridging theory and practice, the Demo Day event included a competition where an evaluation panel of industry and academic experts selected the most innovative startup and best prototype. This competitive aspect not only honed students' business communication skills but also immersed them in situations mirroring the challenges of the real startup ecosystem.

To further reinforce the practical and experiential dimensions of the course, the following digital resources were utilized:

- **Digital Tools for Business Idea Assessment** - Google Trends, Google AdWords, and Uber suggest.
- **Market Research Digital Tools-** Google Keyword Planner, Facebook Audience Insights, Answer the Public
- **Prototype Development-** MIT APP Inventor; Proto.io; Figma (Free starter plan); Looka.com
- **Social Media Advertisement-** Develop social media advertisements on Facebook; Instagram; LinkedIn.

- **Patentability search** - using Google Advanced Patents to verify that your solution has not already been patented.
- **Website development** - WordPress; Jot.com

5. The challenges

This course faced several challenges, including:

- Some students were hesitant to present to external expert audiences.
- Engaging students effectively in Competency-Based Education (CBE) and flipped learning modes.
- Students lacking skills in using technology or software for prototyping.

To address these challenges, the following approaches were implemented:

- Involving students in group activities and encouraging presentations within the class.
- Providing intensive mentoring and coaching to prepare students for pitching to external experts.
- Conducting various workshops during class sessions to train students in using technology and software for developing applications and digital prototypes.

6. How the initiative was received

A satisfaction survey was conducted to gather feedback from student users and participants (see Appendix 1). The results indicate an exceptionally high level of satisfaction among students. They stronglyendorsed this approach, emphasizing its significant contribution to their learning experience and skill development. Notably, the practical components of the course received the highest praise, with students expressing strong enthusiasm in recommending the course to their peers. Appendix 1 contains detailed survey questions, results, and testimonials.

7. The learning outcomes

The core principle guiding the delivery of this course is the Competency-Based Education (CBE) framework, rooted in the constructivist educational approach. This approach asserts that knowledge is constructed through social interaction and shared experiences between learners and experts. To achieve the course learning outcomes, we encourage students to actively engage with their peers and instructor-mentors. This interaction helps students develop entrepreneurial competencies and knowledge, enabling them to apply these skills contextually and appropriately within their respective ecosystems.

To further support the principles of CBE and achieve the course learning outcomes, we have applied the 5E instructional model (Engage, Explore, Explain, Elaborate, and

Evaluate). This model is anchored on the concept that learning should be dynamic and interactive.

Engage: Captivating Interest and Establishing a Supportive Environment
The objective of this element is to enrich the teaching experience and boost student engagement through interactive activities. These activities include role-playing, collaborative learning through group work and projects, and using Lego Serious Play for design thinking and idea generation.

Learning and Teaching Activities Included in the Course:

- **Problem-Based Learning (PBL):** Students will identify various sustainability-related problems. This approach encourages them to apply critical thinking, analyze complex systems, and collaboratively propose innovative solutions and business concepts.
- **Project Work/Group Work (PW):** Students will engage in group assignments and interactive discussions focused on the identified problems. This process leads to the development of sustainable and innovative solutions.
- **Practice-Based Activities (PBA):** Students will apply their acquired knowledge and skills to develop product prototypes. They will present these prototypes to an expert audience for feedback and validation.

Explore: Promoting Active Participation and Collaborative Learning
The learning objective of this element is to cultivate learners' empirical skills and competencies, enhancing their readiness to engage with diverse stakeholders such as investors and entrepreneurs. This is achieved through a series of activities such as Hot-seat pitching events and using course software to develop product concepts and minimum viable products (MVPs). Additionally, prototyping and 1-minute pitches to introduce industry partners were used to spark learners curiosity and inspire informed choices.

Explain: Fostering Critical Thinking
This element of the model was emphasized in every class, with the primary learning objective being to monitor students' participation and guide them in sharing their understanding of various concepts related to the startup development process. Students were encouraged to share their thoughts in an interactive and inclusive manner. To achieve this, students engaged in mini-workshops and seminars they led, presenting identified problems and proposing appropriate tech-oriented solutions that could be introduced to the market as startups. Students were expected to explain their ideas, receive feedback from peers, and collectively refine their business concepts. This process ensured they gained collective validation from both the audience and the instructor-mentor.

Elaborate: Extending Learning and Building Practical Competencies to Establish Startups

The Startup Lab course is a practical, project-based program designed to provide learners with an immersive, applied learning experience. This course guides students through a well-defined process for conceiving and validating innovative business ideas that address real and potential market demands. Through a variety of interactive classroom activities, learners collaborate and cooperate to establish new startups, significantly contributing to their personal growth and self-improvement.

In this collaborative environment, students apply acquired knowledge, skills, and competencies to design prototypes of sustainable products and services aimed at solving community and customer problems. Engaging in group work and embedded projects, students gain hands-on experience that enhances their ability to think critically and strategically.

This structured approach offers learners the opportunity to develop key competencies, including systems thinking, anticipatory skills, critical thinking, strategic thinking, integrated problem-solving, and collaboration. By working together in competency-aware teams, students support each other and collectively work towards innovative solutions, fostering an environment where creativity and innovation thrive.

Evaluate: Assessing Deep Learning and Application Proficiency

A diverse array of assessment and evaluation methods was employed in this course to effectively measure the attainment of the learning outcomes.

1. **How the course learning objectives/ competencies will be assessed:**   2. The module assessment will unfold in the form of a comprehensive portfolio project, structured across three essential steps: 3. **Step 1**: Assignment 1   4. **Step 2**: Assignment 2   5. **Step 3**: A final assessment incorporating two key elements— an individual component centered around the Startup journey Vlog, and a group-based Host Seat Pitching session.
6. **Assignment 1**: In this assignment, students will undertake the challenge of identifying an innovative business concept rooted in comprehensive market research, addressing present market needs. The task involves a thorough analysis, compelling students to articulate how their proposed business concept aligns with the Sustainable Development Goals (SDGs).
Assignment 2: In this assignment, students will undertake the challenge of formulating a comprehensive customer value proposition, creating a storyboard, and developing a prototype for the proposed product or service. This process will seamlessly align with the insights derived from Assignment 1.

7.	**Hot Seat Pitch**: Create a comprehensive slide deck encompassing the elements of an initial business plan with evidence related to the project requirements (business concept development, market research, prototyping, etc.), as well as delivering an effective elevator pitch to persuade an expert audience about the appeal of their business concept.
8.	**Initial Business Plan Portfolio Project**: Group portfolio of an initial business plan with evidence related the project requirements (business concept development, market research, prototyping, etc.)
9.	**The Startup Journey Vlog**: This assignment aims to help students develop their reflective skills, cognitive thinking skills, creativity skills, digital literacy skills and digital presentation skills whilst learning and applying concepts and topics related to Startup creation and development.

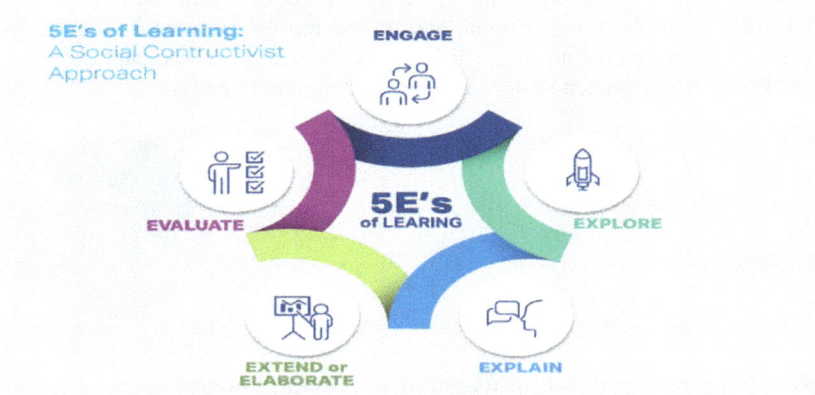

Figure 1. Competency Based Education model (Competency-Based Education @ HCT - Playbook For A Practical Educational Model)

8. Startup Lab Course (ENT 4033) students Satisfaction Survey and feedback

As part of our ongoing efforts to enhance the Startup Lab course content and teaching methods, we conducted a satisfaction survey to gather valuable feedback from students on the course's content, structure, and style. The results indicated a very high level of student satisfaction, with an average rating of 4.91 out of 5 (**Fig.2** Students satisfaction level).

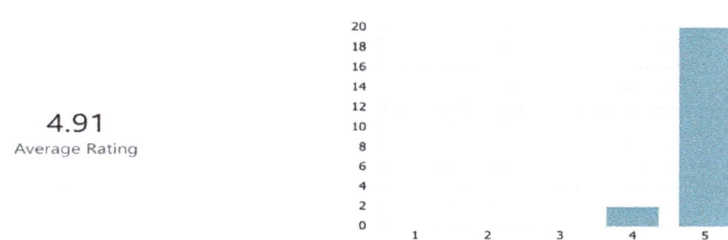

Figure.2 Students satisfaction level

Additionally, learners find the course content, structure, resources, delivery methods, assessments, and the use of technology to be highly relevant and effective. The competency-based approach, in particular, is considered a significant strength of the course (**Fig. 3** Appropriateness for teaching content and material).

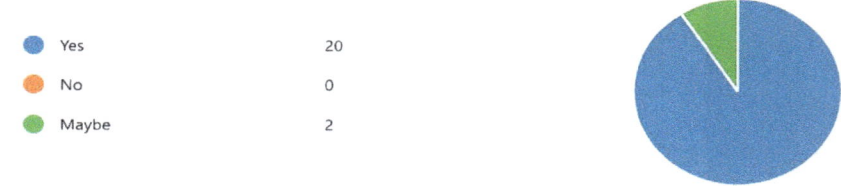

Figure. 3 Appropriateness for teaching content and material.

Students reported that the teaching approach, which emphasized continuous constructive feedback, coaching, and in-class mentoring, was highly effective in enhancing their knowledge, skills, and competencies (**Fig 4**. Teaching approach).

Figure 4. Teaching approach

Regarding the practical component of the course, most students have expressed high satisfaction with the hands-on and experiential elements. This feedback affirms the effectiveness of the Competency-Based Education (CBE) approach implemented in the course. (**Fig 5**. Students' satisfaction on practical content of the course).

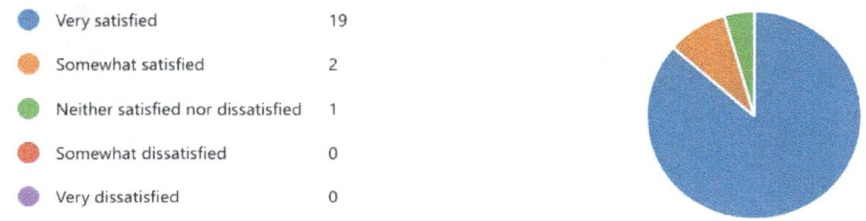

Figure 5. Students' satisfaction on practical content of the course

Students have shown a high level of satisfaction, giving an average rating of 4.82 out of 5 for the appropriateness and effectiveness of the evaluation approach. This approach, which incorporates industry expertise and diverse skills-oriented assessment methods, has been well-received (**Fig 6**. Students' satisfaction on assessment).

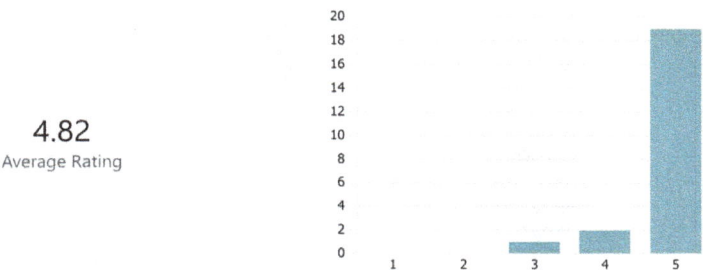

Figure 6. Students' satisfaction on assessment

9. Plans to further develop the initiative.

To enhance this course, one area of improvement is to involve more experts in the student evaluation process. Currently, industry experts participate only in the final stage during the hot seat pitching evaluation. Expanding their involvement throughout the course would provide more comprehensive feedback and mentorship. Additionally, mapping the course content with industry partners such as venture capital firms or business accelerators could be beneficial. This alignment would enable students to join acceleration programs upon course completion, facilitating their entry into the real startup world and providing them with practical support and opportunities for growth.

The 10th Innovation & Entrepreneurship Teaching Excellence Awards

Here is a throwback to the Startup Lab Demo Day events held at Higher Colleges of Technology - Al Ain campus!

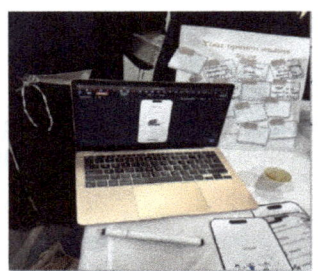

References
Guskey, T. R., & Jung, L. A. (2013). "Competency-Based Education in K–12 Schools: Teachers and Principals as Leaders". Solution Tree Press.

Ford, K. (2014). "Competency-Based Education: History, Opportunities, and Challenges". UMUC Center for Innovation in Learning and Student Success.

Morris, M. H., Kuratko, D. F., & Cornwall, J. R. (2015). "Entrepreneurship Programs and the Modern University". Edward Elgar Publishing.

Klein-Collins, R. (2012). "Competency-Based Degree Programs in the U.S.: Postsecondary Credentials for Measurable Student Learning and Performance". Council for Adult and Experiential Learning (CAEL).

Author Biography

Dr Anji Benhamed holds a Ph.D. from the University of Paris 13, Sorbonne, Paris City, specializing in Strategic Management and Entrepreneurship. She is currently serving as the Business Division Chair (DC) at the Higher College of Technology (HCT) in Al Ain, UAE. With over 18 years of experience in teaching, research, mentoring and consulting across various countries, Dr Anji's contributions extend beyond the academic realm. She is a certified professional Coach-trainer in Entrepreneurship and Leadership, endorsed by the (UNIDO) and the Center for International Private Enterprise (CIPE), USA, (WDI) at Michigan University, USA. She has played a pivotal role as a mentor and coach for startups, collaborating with esteemed business accelerators in the MENA region. Additionally, Dr Anji has served as an external consultant for several companies in the MENA region and internationally.

Entrepreneurship and Innovation: Be inspired

Gaël Bertrand
Full Professor of Entrepreneurship
ESSCA Aix en Provence, France
gael.bertrand@essca.fr

Abstract: The project aims to provide second-year undergraduate students with an introductory experience in entrepreneurship and innovation. By utilizing a hybrid pedagogy, the program transcends common stereotypes, offering both online and in-class learning (see appendix 1 to get an idea of the semester structuration of the course). Students will explore essential tools and concepts such as the Business Model Canvas, pitching, entrepreneurial adequacy, and design thinking. These concepts will be taught online and applied practically in the classroom through direct interaction with entrepreneurs.

Keywords: Entrepreneurship, Hybrid Pedagogy, Blended Learning, Flipped Classroom

1. Introduction: Nature of the course and specific objectives

This course module is designed to give all 2nd year ESSCA students an initial insight into entrepreneurship to initiate and inspire them by addressing the following questions:

- Who are entrepreneurs?
- What is an entrepreneurial project?
- How do you present an entrepreneurial project?
- What is innovation and how innovating and be creative in the entrepreneurial world?

In this course, students interact face-to-face exclusively with real entrepreneurs, founders of their own firms. Academic professors provide the necessary theoretical knowledge through online course videos, equipping students to work effectively with entrepreneurs. The course is designed using a blended learning and flipped classroom learning model, allowing students to grasp entrepreneurship concepts and tools. This approach helps students applying theoretical knowledge practically, leveraging the experience of entrepreneurial professors during face-to-face workshops. The course topics are approached from two different perspectives:

- Firstly, the theoretical and conceptual components of the course, including explanations of various tools, are delivered online and asynchronously (see appendix 3 and look at E-learning sessions). This format provides students with the essential knowledge needed to apply and work on their entrepreneurial projects later. Each online session concludes with students' assignment based

on entrepreneurs' projects, allowing them to immediately put the studied tools and concepts into practice.
- In a second phase, which occurs the following week, a face-to-face session is conducted by a real entrepreneur to review and discuss the students' work from the online session (see appendix 3 and look at workshops sessions). The goal of this session is to apply the concepts discussed in class to real-life scenarios through the entrepreneur's experience, providing students with a practical understanding of entrepreneurship. During the two-hour face-to-face workshops, entrepreneurs evaluate the students' project work and provide valuable feedback. The second part of the workshop is dedicated to applying the concepts and tools studied online, using the entrepreneur's experience to illustrate how these ideas work in practice. This approach helps students gain a deeper, more practical understanding of entrepreneurship.

2. **Topics covered in the course are structured in 3 phases:**
   - The first part of the course focuses on understanding the entrepreneur's career path and entrepreneurial project. This "mirror effect" approach addresses topics such as the entrepreneur's background, the project structuration, and the pitch (see program in appendix, 3).
   - In the second phase, students adopt a theoretical approach to innovation and lean startup methodologies. They are encouraged to innovate by applying the tools they have learned, using these techniques to develop their own projects. This process involves enhancing the entrepreneurial model presented by their entrepreneur-speaker through practical application and project development (see program in appendix 3).
   - The final phase of the course is dedicated to preparing students to pitch their own projects in a major competition organized during the last session on each campus of the school. This phase allows students to challenge each other with their respective projects, gamifying the experience to closely simulate real-life entrepreneurial conditions. This approach helps students refine their pitches and better understand the dynamics of launching an entrepreneurial venture.

The primary objectives of this course are to initiate and inspire students in their entrepreneurial journeys. Additionally, the course aims to identify students who have already started, or are about to start, their own businesses and to support them through the school's entrepreneurship programs. This support may come from the school's incubator, professors, and entrepreneurs involved in the course. From a cross-disciplinary perspective, the ultimate goal is to help students learn and develop the soft skills essential for an entrepreneurial mindset (useful in business world). These skills include public speaking, taking initiative, making proposals, demonstrating leadership, etc.

3. Course originality:

The main originality of the course remain in that the academic part of the course has been based on latest research in the field[1] and practices has been grounded directly through experience of entrepreneurs who are also speakers in face to face with the students.

Moreover, the course's originality has also been based on several other key dimensions:

- **Online, Asynchronous Theory Course:** Students can familiarize themselves with the theoretical content over the span of one week, preparing them for the practical work ahead.
- **Face-to-Face Interaction:** Instead of traditional classroom teaching, an entrepreneur leads the in-person sessions, fostering a stronger and more effective connection between students and industry professionals.
- **Cross-Disciplinary Approach:** The course addresses various dimensions, such as adequacy, ambition, and impactful presentation techniques, which are valuable for both project presentations and job interviews. It also promotes interdisciplinary learning, helping students integrate different management disciplines, like the link between strategy and accounting. Moreover, this course has also been designed to lead students wondering about their own future trajectory, which is the inspiration part of the course. Being guided throughout the semester by an entrepreneur and working directly on the entrepreneur's company prompts students to reflect on their future trajectories, ambitions, and the role of work in their lives. This experience also provides the opportunity to exchange ideas with a notable figure from the business world.

The main challenge is to effectively bridge Theory and Practice. The theory is provided and structured by entrepreneurship professors through online videos and session outlines. The practical application is delivered by entrepreneurs during face-to-face sessions, where theoretical knowledge is brought to life through real-world experiences and storytelling.

4. The infrastructure

To develop this course initiative, we first had to establish both human and digital infrastructure to ensure the content's production for the 1,100 second-year students. Four academic professors specializing in entrepreneurship[2] were initially involved to design the theoretical components of the course, including course materials and videos in both French and English. A pedagogical engineer[3], specializing in Moodle platforms,

---

[1] See appendix 2 for bibliography brief overview
[2] I would like to take this opportunity to express my sincere gratitude for their involvement in this ambitious project. Additionally, I extend my warmest thanks to Professors Xavier Lesage, Laetitia Gabay Mariani, Azadeh Shomali and Brunna Lellis Alcantara.
[3] Laurent Barbin, which is a specialist in new learning technologies and especially Moodle, thank to him for all

was also fundamental to structuring the online portion of the course, ensuring an efficient and user-friendly e-learning path.

Additionally, managing the course during the semester required a robust human infrastructure. To effectively administer the course for the 1,100 participating students, approximately 30 entrepreneurs are recruited "annually" (even if some of them keep on running with us a couple of years) to share their experiences and guide students through the course. Logistically, an administrative assistant is essential on each of the school's seven campuses. These assistants are responsible for planning and organizing the bi-weekly face-to-face workshops throughout the semester, ensuring equitable learning opportunities for all students. Efficient planning and logistics are critical to the smooth operation of the course[4].

5. The challenges

Several challenges were encountered during the development of this course initiative:

Pedagogical Production:
- Lacking specialization in pedagogical video production, we had to learn how to design concise video formats (less than 8 minutes) to effectively convey important concepts, tools, and notions to students asynchronously.
- Additionally, we needed to develop a system on the Moodle platform for exchanging information between students and the professor in charge, allowing us to answer questions related to course content, including videos, support materials, exercises, and assignments.

Bilingual Content Quality:
- Ensuring the course's quality and content in both French and English was essential so that students could participate equally, regardless of language. This included recruiting entrepreneurs capable of teaching in both languages[5].
- Producing and editing videos in two languages was crucial to ensure content was well-presented and engaging for students, requiring us to learn technical aspects of video production.

Moodle Platform Design:
- The technical structuring of the Moodle platform had to facilitate an engaging and efficient online learning path for students.
- The design and ergonomics of the online theoretical course were critical, as usability is a key component of modern e-learning platforms. Although not a

---

[4] I'd like to take this opportunity to thank them warmly for all the behind-the-scenes work (planning, work contracts, etc.) they do on each campus, without which this course simply couldn't run.

[5] A special thanks to Alexandre Tremblay who helped me in the translation of the course in English to get energy in courses' videos especially.

web designer, I had to learn the technical side, with significant assistance from the pedagogical engineer.

According to the latest research on entrepreneurship education (see appendix 2 for an overview of the research bibliography on which the course development is based), especially e-learning, a well-designed user interface is vital for student engagement. This engagement enhances content appropriation, which is crucial for meaningful interactions with entrepreneurs during the face-to-face sessions.

6. Learner Reception and Institutional Impact of the Course Initiative

Learner Reception:
Initially, this initiative surprised learners used to traditional classroom methods. The flipped classroom model, where students learn material before class, presented challenges due to its departure from French educational norms. However, students quickly saw its value, particularly appreciating the direct engagement with real-life entrepreneurs during sessions. This interaction offered practical insights and networking opportunities, including internships, project support, and work-study recruitment. Over time, student reception became even more positive, with feedback consistently highlighting the course's primary aim: to inspire students.

Institutional Impact:
On an institutional level, the program, delivered across seven campuses, including one in Budapest, significantly strengthened ties between students and local entrepreneurial ecosystems. By incorporating local entrepreneurs and other stakeholders into the curriculum, the course provided students with valuable job and internship opportunities. This unexpected outcome underscored the program's effectiveness in integrating students into regional business communities.

Logistically, the initiative successfully managed a multi-campus course for around 1,100 students, ensuring a uniform entrepreneurship experience across six campuses in France and one abroad. This was a significant achievement, given the initial challenge of providing a consistent learning experience across diverse locations.

Educational Outcomes:
Finally, the initiative has had an interesting impact on entrepreneurship education. It demonstrated a novel approach to teaching entrepreneurship by effectively linking theory and practice in a way that resonates with today's learners. The use of modern tools like cell phones and videos made the content more accessible and engaging, aligning with contemporary learning habits. This innovation not only enhanced the educational experience but also established a new way for future courses in entrepreneurship.

7. Impact Measurement of the Course

The impact of the course was assessed from two different perspectives:

Entrepreneurial Intention:
Theoretical Framework: we employed Ajzen's Theory of Planned Behavior (1991) to measure changes in students' entrepreneurial intentions from the beginning to the end of the course. This model helped in understanding the course's influence on students' intentions to pursue entrepreneurship.

8. Course Effectiveness and Student Feedback:
Feedback Collection: During the final session, we measured various aspects of the course to validate its format through student feedback. The following aspects were evaluated:

- Effectiveness of the Course Format: Using 5-point Likert scales (ranging from "extremely ineffective" to "extremely effective"), students assessed group work, program structuring, and the user experience on the platform.
- Richness of Video Content: Students rated the quality and depth of the course videos.
- Knowledge and Skills Acquired: Satisfaction levels regarding the knowledge and skills gained through the course.
- Overall Satisfaction: General satisfaction with the course content.

6.2.1 Survey at the end of the course:

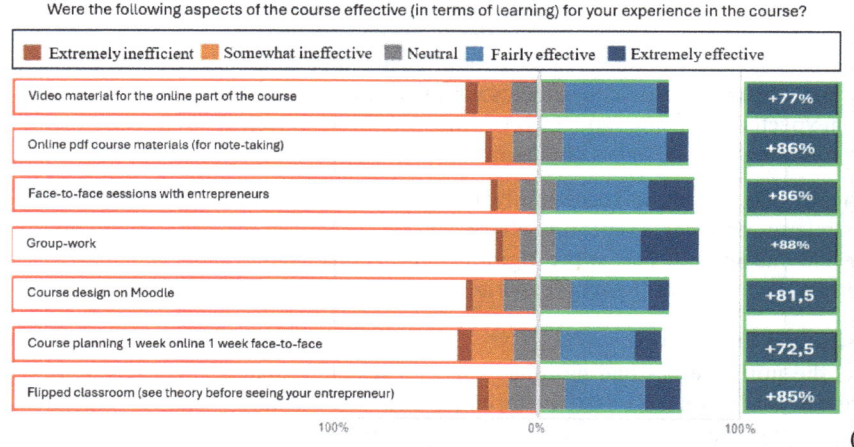

(750 + 600 answers for the 2 last years)

Additional Feedback System:
- The school implemented a comprehensive feedback collection and analysis system at the course's conclusion. This systemic survey invited all students to

provide their opinions, particularly on constructive elements to enhance their learning experience.
- The course was monitored via three web surveys (one at the beginning and two at the end), supplemented by feedback from the entrepreneurs involved.

Key Findings:
- Video Content and Hybrid Format: The quality of the video content, materials, and the hybrid format received an average satisfaction rate of nearly 75%, with some areas identified for improvement in the video materials.
- Entrepreneur-Student Interaction: The strongest aspect of the course was the interaction between students and entrepreneurs, receiving positive feedback from over 92% of participants.
- Flipped Classroom Format: The flipped classroom approach was the most challenging aspect for students to adapt to at the start of the course, as previously mentioned.

Overall, the course has demonstrated significant positive impacts on students' entrepreneurial intentions and has been well-received in terms of content quality and interaction opportunities. Continuous improvements based on feedback will further enhance the learning experience.

9. Plans to further develop the initiative.

Several avenues are currently being explored for continuous improvement of this initiative:

Systematize Statistical Tracking and Feedback: Implement comprehensive statistical tracking of students' interactions on the platform. Regularly survey students to obtain detailed feedback on the content and format, aiming to refine and enhance the course each year.

Enhance Platform Design: Improve the platform's design to make it more intuitive and ensure that online course videos are easily accessible and viewable on smartphones.

Upgrade Course Videos: Revise and improve certain course videos to make them more engaging and enjoyable to watch. Given the importance of video content today, enhancing its quality is crucial for effectively conveying information.

Certain elements can be incorporated into the videos to enhance engagement. For instance, adding a gamification aspect would be highly effective in making learners more active while watching. This could include short quizzes and interactive games developed using H5P technology.

Introduce an Entrepreneurial Marathon: Towards the end of the course, organize an entrepreneurial marathon to provide students with hands-on, practical experience. This will include mentorship from professional entrepreneurial coaches, evaluations by an external jury of specialists, and other activities to closely simulate real-world entrepreneurial challenges.

10. Conclusion

Developing this course has been an incredibly rewarding experience, allowing me to grow as a professor and better understand my students' needs. The goal was to create a course structure that provides a superior learning experience by directly involving entrepreneurs, and this effort has significantly enhanced students' entrepreneurial education.

This initiative also led to the development of a small research program focused on entrepreneurial education, particularly hybrid modalities. This program has resulted in several published papers and acceptance into international conferences, fostering a global network of scholars in entrepreneurial education and drawing inspiration from their insights.

Over the past six years, testing this "centralized" and hybrid flipped classroom format has demonstrated its potential for deployment in specific contexts where the presence of an entrepreneurship teacher is not feasible. For instance, this format can be particularly beneficial in regions with limited logistical access to face-to-face education. By delivering academic content digitally and recruiting local entrepreneurs to share practical knowledge, this approach can foster the development of business start-ups in these often-overlooked areas.

Finally, the achievement I am most proud of is the successful connection established between students and entrepreneurs. This interaction extends beyond the academic realm, enabling students to effectively grasp key concepts and tools in entrepreneurship, as evidenced by their feedback. Moving forward, we aim to enhance this connection by providing students across all campuses with access to diverse entrepreneur perspectives through video testimonials and other mediums.

Additionally, the bonds formed between students and entrepreneurs have proven to be long-lasting in some cases, leading to internships, student contracts, and even student involvement in the entrepreneurs' projects. This enduring impact underscores the success and value of the course. And last but not least, there were also some new entrepreneurs who were inspired by this course, nonetheless, most of the time, we have to wait some years to see them creating their first newly founded firm.

Appendix 1: Structuration of the course through the semester

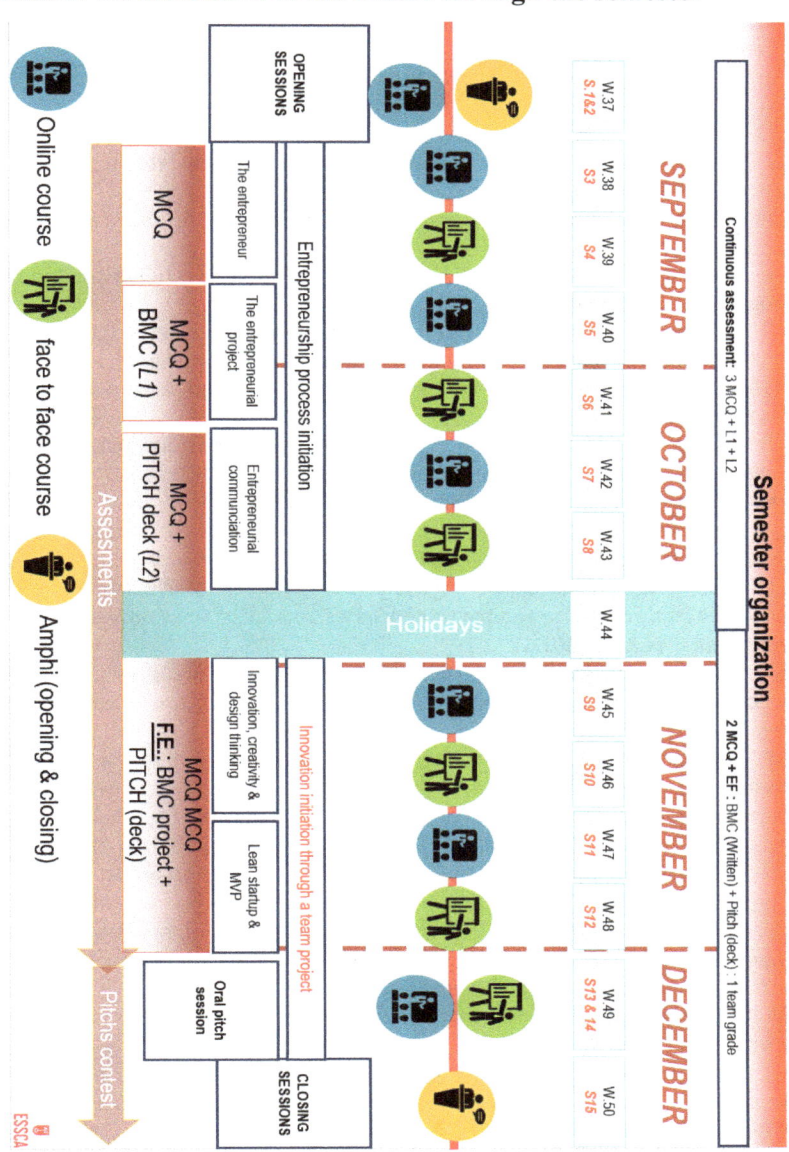

The 10th Innovation & Entrepreneurship Teaching Excellence Awards

Appendix 2: The development of the course is based on a substantial bibliography (brief overview).

Alharbi, J., Almahdi, H., & Mosbah, A. (2018). The impact of entrepreneurship education programs (EEPs) on the entrepreneurial attitudes among higher education students. *International Journal of Management, Economics and Social Sciences*, 7(3), 245-271.

Alshehri, A. F. (2017). Student satisfaction and commitment towards a blended learning finance course: A new evidence from using the investment model. *Research in International Business and Finance*, 41, 423-433.

Ajzen, I. (1991). The theory of planned behavior. *Organizational behavior and human decision processes*, 50(2), 179-211.

Belitski M., Heron K. (2017). Expanding entrepreneurship education ecosystems. *Journal Of Management Development*, 36 (2), 163-177

Bertrand, G., Meunier, L., & Lesage, X. (2022). Is blended learning a magic potion for increasing the entrepreneurial intention of students? 1. Revue de l'Entrepreneuriat, 21(3), 105-138.

Bird, B. (1988). Implementing entrepreneurial ideas: The case for intention. *Academy of management Review*, 13(3), 442-453.

Bird, B., & Schjoedt, L. (2009). Entrepreneurial behavior: Its nature, scope, recent research, and agenda for future research. In A. L. Carsrud, & M. Brännback (Eds.), *Understanding the entrepreneurial mind* (pp. 327-358). New-York, USA: Springer.

Boelens, R., De Wever, B., & Voet, M. (2017). Four key challenges to the design of blended learning: A systematic literature review. *Educational Research Review*, 22, 1-18.

Boissin, J. P., Branchet, B., Emin, S., & Herbert, J. I. (2009). Students and entrepreneurship: a comparative study of France and the United States. *Journal of Small Business & Entrepreneurship*, 22(2), 101-122.

Dziuban, C., Graham, C. R., Moskal, P. D., Norberg, A., & Sicilia, N. (2018). Blended learning: the new normal and emerging technologies. *International Journal of Educational Technology in Higher Education*, 15(1), 3.

Greene, P. G., Rice, M. P., & Fetters, M. L. (2010). University-based entrepreneurship ecosystems: Framing the discussion. In The development of university-based entrepreneurship ecosystems. Global practices. (p. 1-11). Edward Elgar Publishing.

Kautonen, T., Van Gelderen, M., & Fink, M. (2015). Robustness of the theory of planned behavior in predicting entrepreneurial intentions and actions. Entrepreneurship theory and practice, 39(3), 655-674.

Kintu, M. J., Zhu, C., & Kagambe, E. (2017). Blended learning effectiveness: the relationship between student characteristics, design features and outcomes. International Journal of Educational Technology in Higher Education, 14(1), 7.

Liñán, F. (2004). Intention-based models of entrepreneurship education. Piccolla Impresa/Small Business, 3(1), 11-35.

Maalaoui, A., Perez, C., Bertrand, G., & Razgallah, M. (2018). 2" Cruel intention" or" entrepreneurial intention": what did you expect?. *A Research Agenda for Entrepreneurial Cognition and Intention*, 7.

Maalaoui, A., Mejri, C. A., Lahouel, B. B., & Bertrand, G. (2018). De l'audace à l'ouverture au changement des étudiants en école de commerce : une approche de l'intention entrepreneuriale par les valeurs personnelles. Question (s) de management, (1), 103-117.

Mason, J., & Siqueira, A. C. O. (2014). Addressing the challenges of future entrepreneurship education: an assessment of textbooks for teaching entrepreneurship. Innovative pathways for university entrepreneurship in the 21st century, 24, 41-64.

Minniti and Bygrave (2001). A dynamic model of entrepreneurial learning. Entrepreneurship Theory and Practice, 25(3), 5-16

Nadlifatin, R., Miraja, B., Persada, S., Belgiawan, P., Redi, A. A. N., & Lin, S. C. (2020). The measurement of University students' intention to use blended learning system through technology acceptance model (TAM) and theory of planned behavior (TPB) at developed and developing regions: Lessons learned from Taiwan and Indonesia. International Journal of Emerging Technologies in Learning (iJET), 15(9), 219-230.

Rosique-Blasco, M., Madrid-Guijarro, A., & García-Pérez-de-Lema, D. (2018). The effects of personal abilities and self-efficacy on entrepreneurial intentions. International Entrepreneurship and Management Journal, 14(4), 1025-1052. doi:10.1007/s11365-017-0469-0

Toutain, Olivier, Mueller, Sabine and Bornard, Fabienne. (2019)."Decoding Entrepreneurship Education Ecosystems (EEE): A Cross-European Study in Primary, Secondary Schools and Vocational Training." Management International/International Management/Gestión Internacional 23.5

Appendix 3: Topic Program of the course

Every online video course session is ended with a 10 questions and 5 minutes MCQ to ensure that students had effectively followed the online course.

Session 1: Opening session of the course (face to face Session 1, a full face-to-face session is organized on each campus, bringing together all second-year students involved in the course; one session is organized for the French track and another for the English track) Introduction to the course- Presentation of the course (in particular the flipped format and the blended learning dimension of the course), - Testimony of an older entrepreneur - Introduction to the course through the topic: what is entrepreneurship and who are entrepreneurs?

Session 2: (E-Learning Session 1) Course introduction - Presentation of the course (in particular the flipped format and the blended learning dimension of the course), - definition of entrepreneurship and the entrepreneur and a little look at greatest myths around entrepreneurship. This first session has been designed to begin breaking stereotypes about entrepreneurship, especially the famous one best way of the top ten Forbes (where all are men, whites etc.) to enter in the diversity that shape entrepreneurship on the ground.

The 10th Innovation & Entrepreneurship Teaching Excellence Awards
COURSE PART 1 – ENTREPRENEURSHIP THEORY INITIATION

Every theoretical E-learning session will have its own face to face session with an entrepreneur to get the translation of the theoretical session through the experience of a real entrepreneur, to make the bridge between theory and practice and understand what theory cannot transmit yet to student through traditional learning.

Session 3: (E-Learning Session 2) Entrepreneurs and Ecosystems E-Learning video course to better know the entrepreneurs. The course is articulated around the following learning topics:

- Who are they in France?
- What is effectuation and how entrepreneurs work?
- What is an entrepreneurial ecosystem?
- What is intrapreneurship?
- Wondering about the adequacy between people and projects
- Talking about the French dispositive of student entrepreneur status and PEPITES

Session 4: (Face to face Session 2) Workshop 1 - The entrepreneur, who is he/she? Session on the elements that shape an entrepreneur - effectual approach of entrepreneurship - What they see / What they know / Who they know - Exchange with the supervising entrepreneur around the entrepreneur in its broadest sense, his/her history, his/her motivations. Debate around the themes: - How did I fit into my ecosystem? - What link(s) between my business project and my personal life project? (students questioned about this) - How to manage fear and stress? Entrepreneur alone? - What does the entrepreneur think about effectuation? Discussions around the entrepreneur's project so that the students have the elements for the assignments to come on the next course session.

Session 5: (E-Learning Session 3) The entrepreneurial project E-Learning video course to approach topics around the entrepreneurial project like:

- What matters in an entrepreneurial project?
- What is a Business Plan & What are the rubrics of a BP
- Structuring an executive summary,
- How designing the business model canvas

The objective is to reproduce by themselves the business model canvas of the entrepreneurs' project as an assignment (Assignment 1).

Session 6: (Face to face Session 3) Workshop 2 - The entrepreneurial project in practice Debriefing with the entrepreneur of the work submitted (Assignment 1) on the BMC of his/her company. Debate with the students around the following topics (based on storytelling):

- How was the period between the idea and the project, then the reality?
- How to convince the first customers with your value proposition?
- The business planning perspective?
- How did the entrepreneur format its first BMC?

Session 7: (E-Learning Session 4) Communicating in entrepreneurship E-learning video course on business communication and especially on pitching. The course is based on the following topics:
- Entrepreneurial communication
- What is a pitch?
- Which methods for a good pitch?
- Examples of pitches and pitches contests.

The objective is to reproduce by themselves the pitch deck of the entrepreneurs' project as the assignment 2.

Session 8: (Face to face Session 4) Workshop 3 - The pitch Debriefing with the entrepreneur of the work submitted (Assignment 2) on the pitch deck of his company Exchange and debate with the students around the following topics (based on storytelling):
- What context for my first pitch? (issues, why, how it happened etc.)
- How did I practice my pitch?
- What problems did I encounter when pitching?
- How can I improve it?

Announcement of the problem that led the entrepreneur to create his or her company (what needs did he or she seek to meet?): the objective is to get the students to come up with a project idea around this problem in groups for part 2 of the course on innovation.

COURSE PART 2 – INNOVATION AND CREATIVITY INITITATION THROUGH ENTREPRENEURIAL PROJECTS DESIGN

Session 9: (E-Learning Session 5) Innovation, Creativity & design thinking E-Learning video course to better understand the innovation and creativity process and techniques. The course is articulated around the following learning themes:
- What is innovation?
- Introduction to creativity
- What is design thinking?
- The design thinking process and how does it work?

Work on the design thinking method to structure the students' creative process around their own project to design after their own business model canvas and their pitch deck (as their final exam).

Session 10: (Face to face Session 5) Workshop 4 - Innovation and ideation in the entrepreneurial project. Debriefing with the entrepreneur of the work on the students' project and exchange on innovation. This workshop is dedicated to help students' developing their own project business model canvas, through creative and innovation techniques like design thinking. The BMC should be almost finalized at the end of this workshop or at the end of this week.

Session 11: (E-Learning Session 6) Lean startup & MVP to innovate E-Learning video course to understand the challenge of the lean method and mvp to innovate, the course is structured around the following learning topics:

- What is the lean startup?
- The MVP
- What is a pivot?

Student still work on their project to continue developing it through innovation and creative techniques.

Session 12: (Face to face Session 6) Workshop 5 - This workshop is dedicated to look at What is lean startup in practice? Is it necessary to make a pivot? (example with the students' projects that are pivots of the entrepreneur's project).

Debriefing with the entrepreneur of the work on the students' BMC and pitch deck assignment Pitch deck coaching workshop with the entrepreneur, this is the last session before submitting the Business model canvas and pitch deck of students' projects.

COURSE PART 3 – PITCH CONTEST

Session 13: (E-Learning Session 7) Students' pitch work and training E-Learning video course articulated around the following learning themes:

- Reminder on the pitch
- Pitching tips
- Video examples of pitches
- Presentation of entrepreneurship in the school,
- Presentation of existing support and coaching services for entrepreneurial activity in a broader sense (in France).

Session 14: (Face to face Session 7) Workshop 6 - Testing the pitch in real conditions: the pitch challenge, selection of finalists. This last workshop lead entrepreneurs helping their students to finalize their pitch through the first hour. For the second hour of the session, students will have to pitch all (5 minutes max / team) and get Feedback on the pitches to improve for session 15. The entrepreneur makes the selection of the finalists of the pitch challenge for the last session.

Session 15: Closing session of the course (a full face-to-face session is organized on each campus, bringing together all second-year students involved in the course; one session is organized for the French track and another for the English track).) - Testimony of an older entrepreneur (main witness, if possible, an alumni), - Announcement of the finalists of the pitch challenge, - Final of the course pitch challenge (election of the best pitch for each campus by all participants through an online mobile vote). Award for the best pitch of the session for each campus

Author Biography

Gaël Bertrand is Professor of entrepreneurship at ESSCA. He introduces second-year students to the field and manages local entrepreneurial ecosystem connections at the Aix-en-Provence campus. His teaching and research focus on women's entrepreneurship, entrepreneurship education and intention of students, and the survival and performance of newly founded firms.

Connecting Dots: Enhancing Students' Research Skills by Developing Sustainability-oriented Entrepreneurial Projects

Gyuzel Gadelshina and **Nikolaos Goumagias**
Northumbria University, UK
gyuzel.gadelshina@northumbria.ac.uk
goumagias@northumbria.ac.uk

Keywords: entrepreneurship education, learning for sustainable entrepreneurship, research skills

1. Introduction

Entrepreneurship is now recognised as a cornerstone of economic development both nationally and internationally (Carree and Thurik, 2010; Ratinho et al., 2020). The potential of entrepreneurship to solve societal and environmental problems has been widely acknowledged in the literature (Pauceanu et al., 2021). Entrepreneurship education is expected to play a vital role in producing highly skilled, creative, and innovative graduates who can contribute to dynamic changes in social, cultural, and economic environments, address sustainable development issues and respond to labour market challenges (Blesia et al., 2019; Galloway and Brown, 2002). There is a growing body of research investigating the opportunities and challenges of teaching entrepreneurship (Asykin et al., 2019; Mitra and Matlay, 2004). While various specific skills such as problem solving, critical thinking, communication, digital skills, and teamwork are widely discussed in the literature, less attention has been given to the development of research skills in entrepreneurial learning (Hamburg et al., 2019). We seek to contribute to the field of entrepreneurship education by sharing our experience of teaching research skills in the "Entrepreneurial Leadership" module to final-year undergraduate business students at Newcastle Business School (Northumbria University, UK).

2. Required infrastructure for launching the teaching initiative.

"Entrepreneurial Leadership" is a 12-week undergraduate module for third-year business students, taught in the first semester of their final year. The module is designed to support students in learning and developing skills related to the opportunity recognition phase of the entrepreneurial process (Van der Ven and Wakkee, 2004). The term 'opportunity recognition' here encompasses both opportunity creation and identification, although the differences between these concepts are covered in class. Students are required to lead the opportunity recognition process within the entrepreneurial framework and explore the feasibility and sustainability of a social or economic enterprise. Thus, this module aims to develop students' critical thinking and analytical reasoning about sustainable development issues, thereby increasing their awareness of how entrepreneurs can act in a socially responsible manner. The context and structure of the teaching framework are illustrated in Fig. 1.

At the beginning of the module, students are arranged into teams of five and tasked with choosing one of the sustainable development goals (SDGs) that their entrepreneurial project will address. They then develop a business idea aimed at alleviating the chosen SDG. Over the 12-week period, student teams work on their sustainability-oriented entrepreneurial projects which they present for summative assessment. Based on the premise that innovations driving sustainable development "do not necessarily occur by accident" (Schaltegger & Wagner, 2011), students were encouraged to identify, evaluate, and exploit business opportunities that can potentially address the selected SDG by undertaking primary and secondary research. Conducting primary research, such as interviews and surveys is a novel activity for third-year undergraduate business students at this stage. Therefore, the seminar programme in this module is designed to support the teams throughout this challenging process.

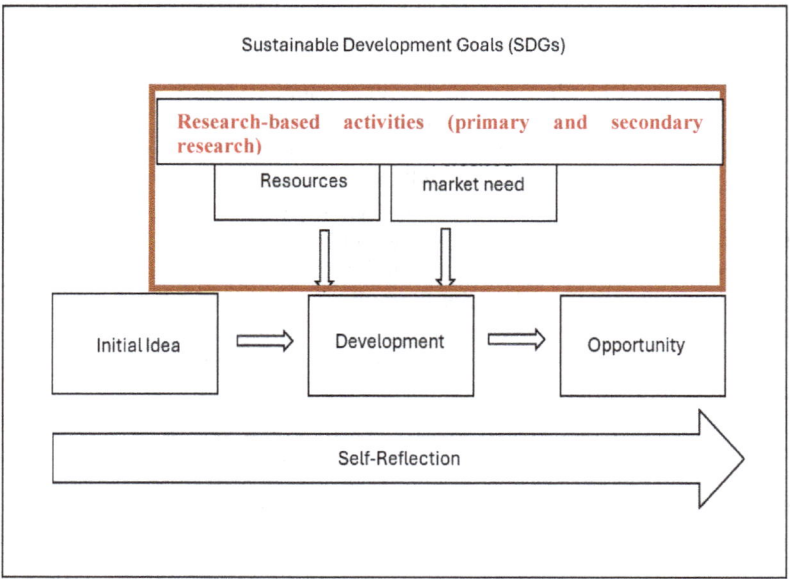

Figure 1 The opportunity recognition process (adapted from Van der Veen and Wakee, 2004) within the module context.

The theoretical aspects of the module are delivered through weekly one-hour lectures. These lectures provide the theoretical foundation for the two-hour seminars that follow, which are designed to emulate the opportunity recognition process outlined in Fig. 1. Seminar activities in weeks 1-7 are structured and led by the tutor. These include various team activities, such as brainstorming sessions and the design sprint process Fig. 2 and Fig. 3. In contrast, seminar activities in weeks 8-11 are led by students, and learning activities are tailored to the stages of their research projects and challenges they encounter as a team. Week 12 seminar is focused on assessment Q&A. To foster the development of research skills alongside theoretical knowledge and to enhance awareness, students are urged to maintain a weekly self-reflection journal to track their skill development process. Crucially, students also receive weekly formative feedback from their seminar tutors.

Regarding the learning outcomes, students are expected to develop their knowledge and understanding of the theoretical aspects of entrepreneurship and enhance a range of transferrable skills. By the end of the module, students should be able to:

- Identify and critically articulate scenarios relevant to opportunities for innovation in sustainable business.
- Understand and critically assess the role of design, innovation, and creativity in new business creation to achieve sustainable solutions.
- Demonstrate key skills and attributes for entrepreneurial effectiveness, including collaboration and entrepreneurial leadership.
- Demonstrate and critically assess an ethical approach to responsible business.

Figure 2 An example of team collaboration exploring the user's journey (Design Sprint).

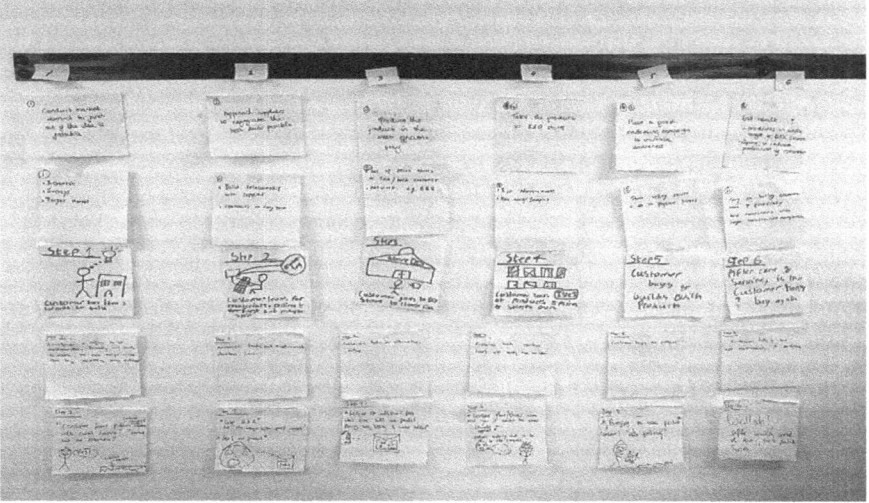

Figure 3 An example of a critical path visualisation (Design Sprint).

Significant emphasis is placed on the ethical aspects of primary research as students prepare to enter the final stage of their studies at university. To uphold the ethical integrity of all the projects, the module teaching process has been approved by the University Ethics Committee. This approval limits the data collection methods available to students to surveys and interviews, both of which are integrated into the module's curriculum. Students are expected to conduct their primary research in accordance with provided guidelines and to adhere to the university's ethical standards. Consequently, this serves as one of the students' initial introductions to the ethical approval procedure which is integral for their final year capstone research project (i.e., dissertation).

The assessment of the module consists of two components: a team presentation (40%) and an individual reflection (60%). The team presentation entails students presenting their business plan to demonstrate how their original idea can be transformed in a sustainable business including a plausible estimate of costs and revenues. The team presentation is structured as follows:

1. A short video (1 – 3 minutes) pitching the entrepreneurial idea to potential investors.
2. A 20-minute presentation followed by 5-minutes Q&A, covering the following points:
   - How the idea has been tested
   - How the idea has been validated
   - - How the project is expected to develop further.

Some examples of students' entrepreneurial projects can be found in Fig. 4.

Also, each student submits an individual reflective statement (1500 words), detailing and discussing their personal experience during the development of the entrepreneurial project. This reflection is related to the individual experience of the student and encompasses the following topics:

1. Entrepreneurial Leadership and Identity
2. Creativity and Design for Innovation
3. Managing Innovation
4. Connectivity and Social Capital
5. Future Search

One key characteristic of the module, communicated clearly to students is the concept of "success through failure". Students are informed that even if their entrepreneurial idea fails, they can still achieve success by demonstrating and discussing their learning journey in the second part of the assessment, i.e. the reflective statement. For our pedagogical project, we collected and analysed 20 reflective statements, totalling approximately 31,700 words. Some of our findings are presented in Table 2 below.

Project "E-CONC

Project "Greenbox Compost"

The 10th Innovation & Entrepreneurship Teaching Excellence Awards

Project "GRILLO"

Figure 4 Examples of sustainability-oriented entrepreneurial projects.

3. Achieved learning outcomes: from learners and participants.

In the final weeks of the module, students were asked to provide feedback on the effectiveness of the teaching and learning process as well as their overall satisfaction with the module. They provided both quantitative and qualitative feedback. Initially, the students were presented with 10 statements and asked to indicate their level of agreement on a 5-point Likert scale. These statements are listed in Table 1. The module survey results, shown in Fig. 5, aggregate responses from two consecutive academic years of module delivery (2021 - 2023). Out of 65 students, 22 responded, resulting in a 33.8% response rate. Overall, the results provide strong evidence of a positive student learning experience.

Table 1 A list of module evaluation survey statements.

	Module evaluation survey statements
Q1	The module was well organised and ran smoothly.
Q2	I felt that the module content was up to date and increased my understanding of the subject.
Q3	I found the module to be intellectually stimulating.
Q4	I have had opportunities to work with other students as part of this module.
Q5	The quality of teaching helped me to learn and enjoy studying the module.
Q6	I have been able to contact/meet module teaching staff when I needed to.
Q7	Learning materials on the module Blackboard site have enhanced my learning.
Q8	The assessment requirements and marking criteria for completion of the module have been made clear and available in good time.
Q9	I have received informative feedback which has allowed me to develop and improve my learning.
Q10	Overall, I am satisfied with the quality of this module.

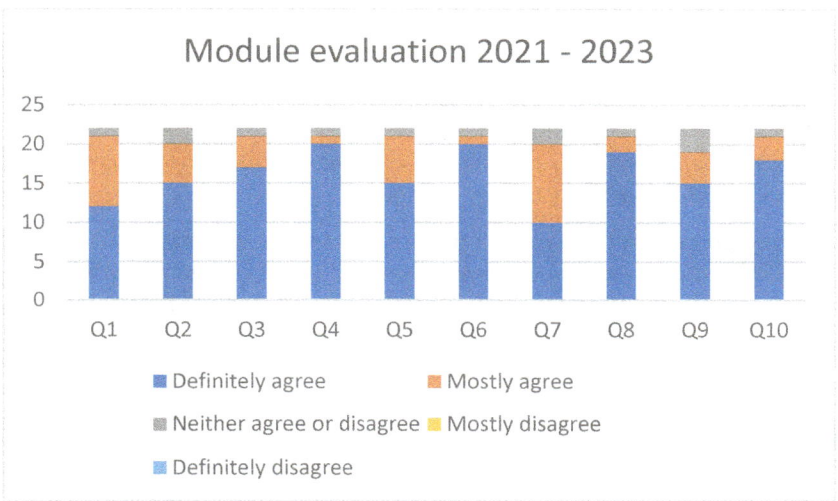

Figure 5 Module evaluation survey between 2021 and 2023 (Note: Students were asked to express their level of agreement on a 5-point Likert scale).

The module survey was supplemented with qualitative feedback, revealing three key themes. Firstly, a positive relationship was identified between the development of transferable skills and overall student satisfaction with the module. Additionally, providing a clear context was important in demonstrating the project's relevance to students, which in turn motivated them to engage more meaningfully with the module.

> "This module felt very relevant, and I feel it has given me real and valuable life skills. It was very hands on and really pushed me to work hard. The teaching was excellent, and it seems everyone was really invested in their project, much like myself. I thoroughly enjoyed this module, it was certainly one of the best modules I've done during my time at Northumbria!"

Secondly, the module successfully promoted group work and significantly contributed to the development of teamwork skills. Students appreciated the collaborative learning environment, as highlighted by the following comments:

> "I liked working with other students in groups to create a presentation, it was a very enjoyable learning environment and kept me interested throughout the module."

> "I enjoyed working in a creative team and being able to just use our own minds and get on with the module without a lot of disruption. I wouldn't improve

anything with the module specifically but perhaps just let students get on with it...".

The third theme highlights the crucial role of tutor leadership in fostering a positive and supportive learning environment. Students particularly valued the tutors' engagement and support, as reflected in the following feedback:

"I thought the teaching [...] was always excellent, specifically the way he would structure the seminars and keep us engaged."

"The best part about the module is our seminar teacher [...]. You can clearly see [they] care[s] about our development and grades as it is reflected in [their] teaching style and support so far throughout the semester. It is personal touches that make [...] lessons so interesting."

4. Challenges and how they were overcome.

While the creation of sustainability-oriented entrepreneurial projects enhanced student engagement with the sustainability agenda and advanced their transferable skills, we observed several challenges that students faced during their projects' development. These challenges can be effectively addressed through the enhancement of their research skills. Identified challenges include:

- Spotting Business Opportunities:
  Some teams encountered difficulties in identifying viable opportunities for their entrepreneurial projects within the context of sustainability.
- Business Idea vs Sustainability-Related Opportunity:
  Some students struggled to distinguish between conventional business ideas and entrepreneurial opportunities aligned with the Sustainable Development Goals (SDGs).
- Abandoning vs Continuing the project:
  Students' teams faced the dilemma of deciding whether to continue pursuing their entrepreneurial project or to abandon it and explore alternative options.
- Lack of Experience and Understanding of Product or Service:
  Many students lacked sufficient experience and understanding of the product or service they aimed to develop in their projects.

These challenges, along with suggested strategies for addressing them, based on the development of research skills, are summarised in Table 2.

Table 2 Challenges encountered during teaching the module and suggested interventions.

Challenges	Examples of students' quotes (reflective statements and module feedback)	Suggested strategies for addressing the challenge
Spotting business opportunities	"…At first, I was trying to lead the group to an idea that I had which was based on saving bees by using wax-coated cloth that would minimise the use of cling film, however, another group member was going towards another business idea which would be cricket powder… my original idea was very different from what our project ultimately turned out to be." "I enjoyed the freedom we had. It resulted in 5 completely different ideas and presentations which is a testament to the freedom we had."	**Dedicated seminar and seminar activities:** This includes structured tutor-led sessions focused on specific topics such as brainstorming, problem mapping, the 5 Whys technique and more. **Discussing examples of secondary research:** This involves exploring various sources of secondary data such as megatrends, inflexion points, and weak signals to enrich the research process.
Business idea vs sustainability-related opportunity	"…I believe that the project was managed through **a continuous drive for creativity**. In the initial stages of the project the entrepreneurial idea was focused on a recyclable vape company however as myself and my peers began to explore more feasible ideas, creative thinking played an important role in the opportunity recognition of a composting business It was apparent that the vape company was insufficient as there were several safety issues. In response, I scheduled a meeting **to brainstorm thoughts and ideas** and this was where GreenBox Compost was born."	**Engagement with primary data collection:** This includes conducting interviews with experts and subsequent discussions with the tutor about the process of data collection and analysis **Development of students' networking skills:** This includes contacting gatekeepers in organisations, managers, experts and students in other schools and faculties.
Lack of experience and understanding of product or service	"the main issue was **a lack of full understanding of the service provided** " "We found from research from the analysis of 101 failed startups' post-mortems that 42% of the reason they fail is that there is **no market need for the product**. That will be the biggest challenge that will emerge in the project's development… "	**Development of understanding of gathering and analysing data**: This includes primary data (e.g., surveys, interviews) and secondary data (e.g., market reports, industry analysis) to gain in-depth insights into market needs and preferences **Exploring various techniques for evaluating entrepreneurial**

The 10th Innovation & Entrepreneurship Teaching Excellence Awards

Challenges	Examples of students' quotes (reflective statements and module feedback)	Suggested strategies for addressing the challenge
		ideas: This involves obtaining feedback from tutors, experts, or potential customers. **Design Sprint.** Development of a toolkit for iterative exploration of the new ideas including envisioning future alternatives, developing prototypes and critical paths, testing and selecting the ideas, collecting feedback. This toolkit allows refinement of ideas to identify the most promising ones. **Developing in-depth understanding of the creative value of entrepreneurial ideas:** This covers aspects of desirability (appeal to potential customers) and feasibility (practicality of implementation).
Abandoning vs continuing project	"...A major challenge that emerged during the project was during our market research. We had the initial idea of surveying people at a D.I.Y store as they are our primary target market. However, we were unsuccessful in contacting managers to ask permission to do this and **had to abandon the idea**. This caused a lot of stress within the team, and almost led to us changing out business idea completely, despite being halfway through the project timeline. After speaking with our seminar tutor and thinking through other options, we came up with an innovative solution to speak to students at Northumbria who study degrees where they would encounter concrete such as architecture and engineering. In the end this worked well as we were able to collect all the data, we needed from people who would actually use the product."	**Exploring data collection challenges:** This includes discussing and addressing issues such as gaining access to gatekeepers, dealing with data saturation, and managing lack of data. **Building understanding of basics of data analysis techniques:** This involves learning methods to extract meaningful insights from collected data. **Continuous weekly tutor feedback:** This feedback includes both detailed (zooming in) and broad (zooming out) perspectives to guide students throughout their projects. **Visualisation of different pathways within the project timeline:** This helps facilitate planning and decision-making.

5. Reflections on the initiative and plans for further development.

Reflecting on our teaching of the "Entrepreneurial Leadership" module, we believe that our innovative project-based approach to teaching research skills through the development of sustainability-oriented entrepreneurial projects provides inexperienced undergraduate business students with a strong foundation for undertaking their final dissertations. Our approach not only has the potential to uncover fresh insights into how research skills support the development of entrepreneurial ideas but also allows students to experience the 'messiness' of the research process. This stands in contrast to the sanitised versions of the research process often presented in research methods textbooks.

Moreover, allowing students to gain firsthand experience with research-based entrepreneurial projects shifts the role of the tutor from merely instructing students to facilitating discussions on challenging topics, such as the failure of business ideas and the roles of leadership and followership in project success. As one student highlighted their team's unique experience, stating: "*...our team decided against having a sole leader. This allowed us to all have ideas and inputs but also take charge of our sectors relative to our skillsets which worked very well for us. ...The leadership was exerted through the team very reasonably as we allowed everyone to do their things, but if there were an issue, then the leader of that sector would fix it. This worked very well and is why we succeeded in the presentation.*"

Finally, we believe that our teaching experience and insights may offer practical value to colleagues who engage in experiential learning, as well as to those who teach research methods and sustainability-related subjects in other educational institutions.

References

Asykin, N., Rasul, M. S., & Othman, N. (2019) 'Teaching strategies to develop technical entrepreneurs', *International Journal of Innovation, Creativity and Change*, 7(6), pp. 179-195.

Blesia, J. U., Iek, M., Ratang, W., & Hutajulu, H. (2021) 'Developing an entrepreneurship model to increase students' entrepreneurial skills: An action research project in a higher education institution in Indonesia', *Systemic Practice and Action Research*, 34(1), pp. 53-70.

Carree, M.A., & Thurik, A.R. (2010) 'The impact of entrepreneurship on economic growth', in: *Handbook of entrepreneurship research*. New York: Springer, pp. 557–594.

Galloway, L., & Brown, W. (2002) 'Entrepreneurship education at university: a driver in the creation of high growth firms?', *Education + Training*, 44(8/9), pp. 398-405.

Hamburg, I., O'Brien, E., & Öz, F. (2019) 'Entrepreneurship & research skills in SMEs', in Dirksen, D. (ed.) *The power of entrepreneurship*. New York: Nova Science Publishers, pp. 45-76.

Jensen, B. B., & Schnack, K. (2006) 'The action competence approach in environmental education', *Environmental Education Research*, 12, pp. 471-486.

Mitra, J., & Matlay, H. (2004) 'Entrepreneurial and vocational education and training: lessons from Eastern and Central Europe', *Industry and Higher Education*, 18(1), pp. 53-61.

Ratinho, T., Amezcua, A., Honig, B., & Zeng, Z. (2020) 'Supporting entrepreneurs: A systematic review of literature and an agenda for research', *Technological Forecasting and Social Change*, 154, p. 119956.

Pauceanu, A. M., Rabie, N., Moustafa, A., & Jiroveanu, D. C. (2021) 'Entrepreneurial leadership and sustainable development - A systematic literature review', *Sustainability*, 13(21), p. 11695.

Ploum, L., Blok, V., Lans, T., & Omta, O. (2018) 'Toward a validated competence framework for sustainable entrepreneurship', *Organization & Environment*, 31(2), pp. 113-132.

Saks, N. T., & Gaglio, C. M. (2002) 'Can opportunity identification be taught?', *Journal of Enterprising Culture*, 10(4), pp. 313-347.

Sam, C., & Van der Sijde, P. (2014) 'Understanding the concept of the entrepreneurial university from the perspective of higher education models', *Higher Education*, 68, pp. 891-908.

Schaltegger, S., & Wagner, M. (2011) 'Sustainable entrepreneurship and sustainability innovation: Categories and interactions', *Business Strategy and the Environment*, 20, pp. 222-237.

Van der Veen, M., & Wakkee, I. (2004) 'Understanding the entrepreneurial process', *Annual Review of Progress in Entrepreneurial Research*, 2(2), pp. 114-152.

Author Biographies

Dr Gyuzel Gadelshina is an Assistant Professor in Strategic Management and International Business at Newcastle Business School, Northumbria University, UK. Her current research explores organisational life using various theories and methodologies from discourse analysis, ethnomethodology and conversation analysis. Gyuzel is a Fellow of the Higher Education Academy (UK) and has a strong interest in pedagogic research, focusing on responsible management education, student learning experience and visual literacy. In 2020, Gyuzel received "Rewarding Excellence in Innovation and Teaching Award" from Northumbria University and won "The Innovation in Teaching of Research Methodology Excellence Award" at the ECRM conference.

Dr Nikolaos Goumagias (Woomayas) is an Assistant Professor at Newcastle Business School of Northumbria University, UK. He teaches Digital Entrepreneurship, Digital Business, and Entrepreneurial Leadership. His research is focused on entrepreneurial finance, venture-capital syndication, business model evolution and digital games industry. Nikolaos obtained his Ph.D. in Applied Informatics (Operational Research) from the University of Macedonia in Greece.

Fostering Innovation Through Integration: The Bath Entrepreneurship Programme's Comprehensive Approach.

Pascal Loizeau
Enterprise Project Coordinator, Bath Enterprise
Entrepreneurship Programme, University of Bath, UK
pl246@bath.ac.uk

1. Introduction

This case history explores the University of Bath's strategic approach to teaching entrepreneurial and intrapreneurial skills, with a focus on the integration of the Intrapreneurial Knowledge Exchange Enterprise Pathway (IKEEP) into the Bath Entrepreneurship Programme. The initiative aims to boost student engagement with start-up services, cultivate innovation, and offer practical, real-world experiences. This document outlines the objectives, infrastructure, and challenges of the merged programme, as well as its reception, learning outcomes, and future development plans. By examining the successes and lessons learned from this integration, we aim to provide valuable insights for other institutions seeking to enhance their entrepreneurship education offerings.

The Bath Entrepreneurship Programme is an extracurricular initiative that students choose to participate in alongside their academic studies. At its core, our Entrepreneurship Programme, augmented by INTRA is more than just a curriculum. By delivering practical know-how, fostering a culture of innovation, and providing hands-on experience, it's a launchpad for future innovators and change-makers. This initiative aligns with the broader educational mission of seamlessly integrating theoretical knowledge with practical experience, equipping individuals with the tools to navigate the complexities and uncertainties of the modern business landscape.

The key objectives of the merged initiative include:

- Enhancing engagement with startup services and addressing government priorities related to entrepreneurship and innovation.
- Promoting an entrepreneurial mindset through intrapreneurial experiences.
- Fostering a capacity for change across all academic disciplines.
- Cultivating a collaborative and innovative environment that values diversity and encourages cross-pollination of ideas.

The 10th Innovation & Entrepreneurship Teaching Excellence Awards

Pitching workshop 'Pitch Perfect'

2. Infrastructure

As part of the Research and Innovation Service (RIS) department, the Student Enterprise team has access to a broad range of expertise and resources, such as intellectual property (IP) guidance and other resources offered by RIS and the university.

People

Student Enterprise play a crucial role in coordinating and executing various aspects of the pedagogical initiative. The dedicated team includes:

- • One full-time staff member, responsible for overseeing the day-to-day operations and strategic planning of the initiative.
- • A part-time staff member, responsible for inbound and outbound marketing.
- • A staff member, on a 12-month funded contract, responsible for the Intrapreneurial Knowledge Exchange (INTRA).
- • A former student who devotes approximately 10 hours per week to collect data and provide invaluable students insights.

Resources:

Access to suitable physical spaces, collaborative workspaces and meeting rooms are crucial for facilitating hands-on learning experiences and fostering collaboration among participants. The University of Bath provides a dedicated space equipped with state-of-the-art facilities to support the initiative's activities and accommodate the diverse needs of participants. Curating and providing access to online resources, including articles, case studies, videos, and interactive tutorials, enriches the learning experiences of participants. These resources supplement workshops and master classes, offering flexibility, accessibility, and self-paced learning opportunities to accommodate diverse learning preferences and schedules. Additionally, the use of social platforms not only facilitates communication and collaboration but also enhances the overall learning experience and prepared students for the digital landscape of modern entrepreneurship.

Sales & Marketing workshop

We assess our programme effectiveness through multiple channels. Students and company hosts provide feedback via surveys and cards. Additionally, we conduct pre- and post-training questionnaires to gauge students' career aspirations, including interest in entrepreneurship. Placement data is collected throughout the academic year to measure programme impact.

Partnerships:

Collaboration with external partners is crucial to the success and sustainability of the programme. By partnering with incubators, innovation hubs, and financial institutions, participants gain access to resources, networks, and opportunities beyond the university campus. These partnerships facilitate experiential learning, mentorship, and access to funding and support services for aspiring entrepreneurs, aligning with the university's commitment to making a positive impact with the wider community.

Student societies, such as Bath Entrepreneurs play a vital role in fostering a culture of innovation and entrepreneurship on campus. These societies are a valuable source of engaged and motivated students who are eager to develop their entrepreneurial skills. These societies feed into our initiative, providing us with a steady stream of motivated and talented students. In turn, we offer support and mentorship.

Individualised mentorship and coaching sessions connect participants with experienced entrepreneurs, industry professionals, and academic advisors. These mentors provide one to one guidance, feedback, and support tailored to the students' specific needs and aspirations. Mentorship relationships foster personal and professional growth, expand networks, and increase confidence and resilience in participants as they navigate the entrepreneurial journey. Alumni of the programme are also invited to give by sharing their entrepreneurial journeys, providing valuable insights and inspiration.

Networking events, peer-to-peer interactions, pitching opportunities, and other activities create opportunities for participants to connect, collaborate, and share experiences with like-minded individuals. Building a supportive and inclusive

The 10th Innovation & Entrepreneurship Teaching Excellence Awards

community fosters a culture of innovation, collaboration, and mutual support, enriching the learning and growth experiences of participants.

3. Challenges

To address the challenges posed by the academic calendar our entrepreneurship programme is designed with flexibility and strategic timing in mind. We understand that periods such as December to early February and the entire month of May are not feasible for extracurricular activities due to exams and revision time. Therefore, we've structured the programme around less demanding times of the academic year, ensuring minimal disruption to students 'studies.

We are particularly focused on increasing STEM student participation in our entrepreneurship programme. To this end, we are emphasizing benefits that are especially attractive to this demographic, such as hands-on experience with cutting-edge technologies and exposure to innovation-driven companies.

Our commitment to flexibility and strategic timing extends to all aspects of the programme, including the integration of the Intrapreneurial Knowledge Exchange Enterprise Pathway (IKEEP). Originally, IKEEP received £2 million in funding across five universities for a two-year period from 2021 to 2022. Recognising its success and value, we have integrated IKEEP into our entrepreneurship curriculum. This expansion allows us to reach a broader range of students while retaining the core principles of skill-building for employability.

By incorporating IKEEP, now rebranded as INTRA, we offer a comprehensive entrepreneurial experience. We have revamped marketing materials and optimised administrative processes with partner organisations to support this expansion. Tailored marketing campaigns have been launched to attract students from diverse academic backgrounds, emphasizing the value of entrepreneurial skills across all disciplines.

Our involvement in this process is complex and varied. We work with local businesses to create engaging projects, promote INTRA, and involve students in online training. We then match students with suitable organisations based on their skills and interests and provide ongoing support throughout each project. A contract binds the students and the organisations involved. Operating this programme with a small team is challenging, especially since many startups we engage with are often run by only one or two people, requiring significant time commitment from us to assist them effectively.

The careful alignment of SME requests with student availability, considering the academic calendar, has been crucial to the programme's success. This approach ensures that both students and businesses benefit optimally, despite the varying demands of the academic year.

While INTRA projects are unpaid, they offer substantial value through practical experience and networking opportunities. The lack of financial compensation presents a significant challenge, potentially limiting participation from students who need to prioritise paid work. However, we've designed the programme to emphasize long-term benefits that offset this short-term financial consideration:

4. Long-term Benefits of the Programme:
1. Real-world Experience: Students gain hands-on experience working with actual businesses, providing a competitive edge in the job market.
2. Skill Development: Participants develop crucial entrepreneurial and intrapreneurial skills that are highly valued across industries.
3. Network Building: The programme offers opportunities to build professional networks with industry leaders, startups, and fellow entrepreneurs.
4. Career Exploration: Students can explore different industries and roles, helping them make informed career decisions.
5. Portfolio Enhancement: Completed projects serve as tangible evidence of skills and experience for future job applications.
6. Digital Badges and Certifications: These provide recognised credentials that enhance employability.
7. Potential Job Opportunities: Successful placements can lead to job offers or long-term collaborations with participating companies.
8. Entrepreneurial Mindset: The programme cultivates an entrepreneurial mindset that is valuable in any career path.
9. Cross-disciplinary Collaboration: Working in diverse teams enhances students' ability to collaborate across different fields.
10. Innovation Skills: Students learn to identify opportunities and develop innovative solutions, skills that are increasingly important in today's rapidly changing job market.

By highlighting these advantages, we aim to show that, despite being unpaid, the projects provide significant value for students' future careers. This approach addresses the financial challenge while showcasing the programme's benefits, especially for STEM students seeking to boost their entrepreneurial and technical skills.

5. Enrolment and Engagement Metrics

The entrepreneurship programme, valued for its hands-on experience, has seen significant engagement with 680 students from 72 different courses. Throughout the year, 45 events were hosted, 294 hours of knowledge exchange where delivered, attracting 473 attendees. The student body is diverse, with nearly half being postgraduates (48.2%) and the rest undergraduates (51.8%). Academically, students come from Science (17.9%), Humanities and Social Sciences (15%), Engineering and Design (21.4%), and the School of Management (45.7%).

INTRA surveys gauge satisfaction, project outcomes, skills rating, learning outcomes, and improvement suggestions.

- 48 students completed the INTRApreneurship training. (118 students enrolled).

- 77% Badge Acceptance rate (Credly average is 67%)
- 8 Startups, 1 SME, and 4 student-led startups.
- 39 students participated in the INTRApreneurship experience. INTRA(X).

After the placement, students are invited to participate in a survey, giving them the opportunity to reflect on their journey. We also seek feedback from businesses to ensure continuous improvement. This real-life project experience can sometimes lead to job opportunities for students. The fact that companies often participate repeatedly is a testament to the value they derive from this collaboration.

Qualitative Metrics : Testimonials from SMEs:
Wavesix Ltd - Go to Market Strategy in the US
"It was great to see how willing the students were to embrace the project. They were happy to set up meetings and organise themselves. They all have a solid understanding of research and presenting their findings, requiring minimal guidance in these aspects. I learned that having a strong brief from the outset is crucial."

- Julia M. CEO and Founder

TILIAN Kids - Launch of a New Service
"Students allocated tasks based on their skills and experience, and this approach worked very well from our perspective. Hopefully, they learned about some of the practical issues associated with running a small business. This was their first exposure to retail, and we hope they gained much from getting a discrete project off the ground."

- Paul M. CEO and Co-founder

FRAMESports.ai - Financial Projection to Raise Money
"The students totally matched my expectations. I set tasks at the beginning of the week, we agreed on deadlines, and then worked around them. They had a basic understanding of financial reporting, which helped tremendously."

- Lachlan M. CEO and Founder

6. Feedback from Students:
Jessica P.- MSci Sport and Exercise Science, Placement with FRAMESports.ai
"This experience surpassed my expectations. I gained extensive knowledge about the financial aspects of start-up businesses, including the creation of a Total Addressable Market (TAM) document for investors. I collaborated effectively on a financial projection report. The communication work proved to be especially valuable with the placement being remote. I now feel more confident about pursuing opportunities in other industries and realise that I am not restricted by my degree."

Priya N. - BSc International Management - Placement with Wavesix
"The placement matched my expectations very well regarding the tasks and the end report and presentation we had to make. I did not know we would have daily stand-up meetings, but I really liked them as they gave good structure to the four-week placement. I developed an intrapreneurial mindset, trying to come up with new ideas to improve the project. I contributed by thinking of different ways the app could stand out or succeed if it entered the US market. I learned valuable presentation tips from other team members, which I will use in my future courses. I also improved my time management skills through the daily stand-up meetings and realised the value of voicing my ideas."

Eunjong K.- BSc Politics and International Relations – Placement with EDEN
"I expected the placement to be like a uni's team project, but I was surprised to find it was a professional and excellent activity."

Josh M.- MEng Aerospace engineering - LinkedIn
"As I look back on these five years, I am grateful for the support of all my friends and family, alongside all of the *opportunities available outside of engineering including being the treasurer for the photography society and completing the entrepreneurship program from Enterprise Bath*."

Yothin L. – MSc Strategic Retailing - LinkedIn
"To all my connections, if you're a student or just someone eager to dip your toes into the realm of entrepreneurship, I strongly recommend keeping an eye on Enterprise Bath's offerings. These events are not merely sessions; they're transformative experiences."

7. Areas for improvement highlighted by students:

"The most challenging experience in the project was communicating across different members and organising a suitable time that is suitable for all of us."

"I like how we were learning about how to move the company forward. However, there was a lack of tasks and it did not reach the hours that I expected to work for."

"Four weeks is not sufficient for us to have a deep understanding of the company. Hopefully next time we can learn about the company better (or get a company brief a week before the project actually starts."

"Since it's a remote programme, the communication didn't go quite smoothly as we were all in different time zones and in-person meeting wasn't an option. Also, due to the time limit, we were not able to understand the objectives and the company in general. It would be better if the length of this programme could be extended to 8 weeks with some kind of stipend."

8. Learning outcomes

Innovation is paramount within higher education where commercialising research findings and entrepreneurship is key. Unlike traditional academic offerings, our programme focuses on experiential learning, allowing students to apply new knowledge in real-world scenarios.

Recognising that entrepreneurship is a way of thinking and to captivate students beyond their academic commitments, the programme engages them through interactive workshops and training sessions, moving away from passive lectures. This approach encourages active participation while imparting essential knowledge and skills, helping them to develop an entrepreneurial mindset for success. Active learning fosters greater engagement and enthusiasm enhancing information retention and understanding.

Practical exercises allow students to apply theoretical knowledge to real-world scenarios, enhancing their problem-solving and critical thinking skills, with immediate feedback from peers and facilitators refining their ideas and approaches. Hands-on activities encourage creative thinking and innovation, essential traits for successful entrepreneurs, and provide a safe space to experiment and take risks, building resilience and adaptability.

Collaborative tasks promote teamwork and communication skills, mirroring real entrepreneurial environments, and offer networking opportunities with peers, mentors, and industry professionals. By demonstrating the real-world relevance of entrepreneurship, students are more motivated to pursue their ventures, and exposure to successful entrepreneurs can provide inspiration and role models. These sessions also build self-confidence and a sense of achievement, developing essential leadership skills.

Intended learning outcomes:

- Develop an entrepreneurial mindset.
- Gain practical experience in applying business concepts to real-world scenarios.
- Enhance problem-solving and critical thinking skills.
- Improve teamwork and communication abilities.
- Learn to create business models and strategies.
- Understand innovation management.
- Develop leadership skills.
- Gain knowledge in diversity and inclusion in a business context.
- Learn to pitch business ideas effectively.
- Understand the process of developing a minimum viable product (MVP).
- Gain experience in market research and customer segmentation.
- Develop project management skills.

The Entrepreneurship Programme covers a comprehensive range of topics, including problem and opportunity identification, idea generation, hypothesis and validation, lean canvas, business model development, market research, customer segmentation, IP, marketing strategy, business plan creation, building a minimum viable product (MVP), equity strategy, and several pitching sessions.

Throughout the programme, participants gain practical tools and strategies for launching and scaling their ventures. This is complemented by several competitions in the 'Dragons' Den' style and funding opportunities. The Innovation Award competition is open to final-year students with scalable projects aligned with the university's beacons: Health and Wellbeing, Sustainability, and Cyber and Digital.

We actively seek business projects for our students to undertake, providing them with the opportunity to act as intrapreneurs/consultants and gain invaluable experience. In return, the participating companies serve as mentors, guiding the students through real-world challenges. Companies understand the value of fresh talent and innovative perspectives, and we believe that partnering with organisations offers our students invaluable learning experiences.

INTRA consists of two main components: online training and practical application.

Phase 1: Online Training

The online training phase engages students in a comprehensive curriculum covering essential skills such as business modelling, critical thinking, effective communication, and problem-solving. Upon completion, students earn a digital badge recognising their achievement. To provide a more familiar and robust learning environment for students while enabling better progress tracking, we're transitioning the content from Microsoft Forms to Moodle (Bath University's LMS).

The first 80% of the online INTRApreneurship training programme consists of six graded chapters:

1. Introduction to Intrapreneurship (7 points)
2. Innovation Management (9 points)
3. Business Modelling & Strategy (5 points)
4. Communication (17 points)
5. Leadership & Management (10 points)
6. Diversity & Inclusion (5 points)

Students can complete these at their own pace, over two weeks, which includes recorded content, supplementary reading, and short reflective answers. This takes approximately 8 to 10 hours of effort. The remaining 20% of the programme is a 2-hour online Zoom session, necessary to complete the training and recap the learning outcomes.

Phase 2: INTRA(X) Practical Application

Following the online training, INTRA(X) offers a flexible, project-based experience. This phase is optional and allows students to collaborate on diverse ventures, partnering with external startups and SMEs or accelerating advanced student-led initiatives, providing opportunities to find potential co-founders and collaborators.

The 10th Innovation & Entrepreneurship Teaching Excellence Awards

INTRA(X) offers short, remote project placements with regional businesses or the option for students to pursue their own developed projects. These four-week, 70-hour projects involve interdisciplinary teams of three students, fostering a dynamic peer-to-peer learning environment. Students apply their skills in real-world challenges, build meaningful connections, and address knowledge gaps within their teams. Projects yield tangible results such as market studies, product strategies, and financial projections, but the initiative is open to exploring other project ideas that align with business objectives.

The programme welcomes project proposals from a wide range of organisations, including local SMEs, startups, charities, non-profits, social enterprises, and retailers. This inclusive approach allows students to gain exposure to diverse industries and contribute to organisations with varying objectives.

Through the placement component of the curriculum, students gain valuable real-world experience and direct access to the CEO, boosting their confidence and providing a unique opportunity to learn from seasoned business leaders. This experience allows students to refine their skills in time management, project management, and group dynamics, while also gaining new perspectives, innovative solutions, and forging valuable industry connections.

The interdisciplinary team composition is particularly beneficial when there is a strong technical project but a lack of commercial expertise, or vice versa. By leveraging each other's strengths, students can learn from one another while accommodating various schedules and commitments. This approach ensures that each project team is well-rounded and capable of tackling the multifaceted challenges of entrepreneurship. Whether working with local SMEs or on their own projects, students gain valuable experience and insights that prepare them for future entrepreneurial endeavours.

INTRA(X) is particularly well-suited for early-stage businesses seeking fresh perspectives and innovative solutions. Projects can encompass key strategic initiatives that may have been on hold or require new ideas to propel them forward. Given the condensed timeline, it is crucial to design projects with realistic deliverables that can be accomplished within the specified timeframe. Flexibility is key, and students can explore additional tasks if they complete the primary objectives ahead of schedule.

Engaging in real-world projects offers students invaluable insights into the challenges faced by companies and fosters a deeper understanding of the business landscape. The initiative recognises students' achievements through two digital badge certifications. The first badge is awarded upon completion of the self-study on intrapreneurship, and a second digital badge by successfully completing a project placement.

The experiential project experience involves three cohorts of students, with the placements scheduled in Autumn, Spring, and Summer to avoid conflicts with holidays and exams. During their internship, students may be in different time zones, and they will need to learn to collaborate effectively across geographical boundaries.

The placement's emphasis on teamwork and collaboration promotes a cooperative environment, while the focus on problem-solving and adaptability equips students to tackle the challenges of the modern business landscape. Even if students decide not to create their own business straight after graduation, the commercial awareness gained from this experience gives them an added advantage in their future careers.

As a crucial part of the internship experience, we highly recommend that projects conclude with a final presentation or report. This presentation highlights the students' work, the methodologies they used, and their recommendations for the organisation's benefit. We believe that aligning project expectations and ensuring a mutually beneficial collaboration is essential.

Students must fulfil the following requirements to obtain the Enterprise Certificate: complete at least five workshops, collaborate with a mentor to develop a business idea, deliver a persuasive pitch to our expert panel, and participate in an INTRA(X) project.

One aspect we need to explore further is the low rate of students showcasing their awarded badges on LinkedIn. This trend may be attributable to students not extensively using LinkedIn for their CVs or to highlight their achievements. Interestingly, even the mention of their graduation on this platform is relatively low. Understanding this behaviour is crucial for us, as it can help us better support students in promoting their accomplishments and leveraging professional networks effectively. We may need to provide more guidance on the benefits of using platforms like LinkedIn for career advancement or explore alternative platforms where students might be more actively engaged.

While our current evaluation methods offer valuable insights, we recognise opportunities to enhance our assessment of teaching outcomes. To this end, we plan to implement longitudinal studies, tracking programme participants over extended periods to evaluate the long-term impact on their careers and entrepreneurial activities. This approach will provide more robust evidence of the programme's effectiveness. Additionally, we aim to engage in peer benchmarking, comparing our programme's outcomes with similar initiatives at other institutions. This will help us gauge our relative performance and identify areas for improvement. Lastly, we're committed to developing a more comprehensive alumni network. This robust system will allow us to better track and engage with programme graduates, gathering crucial long-term impact data and ensuring we deliver lasting value to our participants.

9. Plans to Further Develop the Initiative

To drive further development, we are intensifying our efforts to engage students from all academic disciplines and backgrounds. This will involve targeted marketing and outreach programmes across university faculties and departments to showcase the initiative's benefits.

The 10th Innovation & Entrepreneurship Teaching Excellence Awards

Alumni and mentors have found the experience enriching, both in terms of giving back to the university community and gaining fresh insights from current students. The collaborative environment fostered by the programme has been noted as a significant strength. Our expertise is recognised, and we are frequently invited by departments with entrepreneurship curricula to contribute to panels and discussions, establishing ourselves as the entrepreneurial hub at Bath.

Access to practical knowledge and professional networks equips students to navigate challenges, explore opportunities, and make informed decisions as they embark on their entrepreneurial journeys. The team recognises the value of creating a bounded community where participants can thrive and build lasting relationships.

Seeking additional funding and mentorship opportunities is crucial to support a growing number of participants.. We have received requests from organisations to source students with expertise in deep tech areas such as Artificial Intelligence, Engineering Biology, Telecommunications, Semiconductors, and Quantum Technologies. To meet this demand, we are exploring ways to connect with students who have the required skills and knowledge and provide them with opportunities to apply their expertise in real-world challenges while maintaining the entrepreneurial mindset.

Continuous evolution is key to cultivating the entrepreneurial spirit among students. The initiative will adapt to incorporate industry trends and demands, developing new training modules and project placements to remain relevant and impactful in an ever-changing landscape. While we support startups, we also value diverse business paths and new SMART goals will be defined for each area of development.

Efforts to streamline administrative tasks, such as attendance and data collection, through automation will enhance efficiency and reduce costs. As the programme's success grows, careful planning and resource management will be essential to maintain quality while scaling operations. We aim to introduce a marketplace system that allows students to select projects based on their interests and availability, ensuring a tailored experience and evidence of impact for university stakeholders.

Our programme is also designed to provide international students with valuable experience and credentials that can support their applications for the Global Talent Visa. This visa is particularly beneficial for founders and employees with technical or business backgrounds, covering various tech sub-sectors. The visa allows holders to be self-employed for up to 5 years, with the option to extend or apply for permanent settlement in the UK. For master's students, whose academic year often concludes in September, the summer months offer a perfect opportunity to engage in project-based experiences.

We are excited to expand our horizons through international collaborations, which will open new avenues for knowledge exchange and cross-cultural entrepreneurial experiences. These partnerships go beyond academic exchanges, providing our students with global perspectives on entrepreneurship. We are exploring possibilities for student exchanges, joint projects, and virtual collaborations to enrich the entrepreneurial journey for students at all participating institutions.

While these international collaborations are in the early stages, we are enthusiastic about their potential. We are thoughtfully considering how to leverage these relationships to enhance our programme and provide our students with valuable international exposure. These partnerships align with our goal of preparing students for the global business landscape they will enter upon graduation, and they will help elevate our university on the international stage.

10. Conclusion

The Enterprise Bath Entrepreneurship Programme stands as a beacon of collaboration, diversity, and innovation in the educational landscape. By integrating entrepreneurial and intrapreneurial skills, the initiative has not only equipped students with practical knowledge but also instilled a mindset of adaptability and resilience.

The programme's emphasis on experiential learning and real-world application ensures that students are active participants in their entrepreneurial journey, fostering risk-taking and creativity within a supportive environment. This approach is cultivating a new generation of innovative thinkers and doers.

Looking ahead, the initiative's plans for further development and expansion underscore its commitment to nurturing the entrepreneurial spirit across all academic disciplines. By embracing diverse perspectives and forging strong partnerships with industry leaders and alumni, the Enterprise Bath Entrepreneurship Programme is poised to continue shaping the future of entrepreneurship both within and beyond the university community.

In essence, the Enterprise Bath Entrepreneurship Programme exemplifies the university's dedication to empowering individuals to thrive in an ever-evolving business landscape. With a focus on innovation, collaboration, and real-world experiences, the initiative remains at the forefront of preparing students to become effective agents of positive change.

By 2028, Enterprise Bath aims to be recognised as a leading hub for Early Career Researchers and student entrepreneurs in the UK, fostering a thriving ecosystem that empowers them to transform innovative ideas into successful ventures. This vision will position the University of Bath as the top choice for entrepreneurially minded individuals.

The 10th Innovation & Entrepreneurship Teaching Excellence Awards
Appendix: Student Startups

Business	Description	Category	Alumni Innovation Award	Further Funding	MVP	Sales £
Estudiamos	Self-marking revision tool for language students.	Tech	Yes	Yes	Yes	Yes
Vibestride	AR gaming boosts girls' PE engagement.	Tech	Yes	Yes	No	No
Taigh Companion	IoT-powered smart home care solutions.	Tech	Yes	Yes	Yes	Yes
FrameSports.ai	AI-powered video analysis for rugby.	Tech	Yes	No	No	No
Moored Solutions	Online and on-site mooring bookings and payments.	Tech	No	Yes	Yes	Yes
The Green Co.	Innovating compact, eco-cleaning solutions.	Sustainability	No	Yes	Yes	Yes
Vycto	Gamifies sports sponsorships for ROI.	Tech	No	No	No	No
UniCritters	Campus fashion, sustainably sourced.	Fashion	No	No	No	Yes
SignaChip	Motor controller powers electric vehicle.	Tech	No	No	No	No
Moodmetrics.ai	Forecast finance with AI and public sentiment.	Tech	No	No	Yes	No
Bizware	Affordable, customizable cloud ERP for SME growth.	Tech	No	No	No	No
Coldleady	AI-powered lead qualification for digital agencies.	Tech	No	No	No	No

The Mach Cup	International University RC Aircraft Speed Competition event.	Tech	No	No	No	No
Stinki	Affordable, functional male fragrance for Gen-Z.	Fashion	No	No	No	No
NavBots Robotics	SAAS for warehouse robotics.	Tech	No	No	No	No
UppyThings	Upcycling building wraps into sustainable products.	Sustainability	No	No	Yes	No
YGY	Empowering young people through education and mentorship.	Social	No	No	No	No
LineUp	SAAS for ticket booking, resale, and payment management.	Tech	No	No	Yes	No
MET	AI-powered capture and analysis conversations for smarter connections.	Tech	No	No	No	No
Campus Compass	Real-time campus data for smarter student experience and campus efficiency.	Tech	No	No	Yes	No
Bored of Boards	3D printed maps and game boards for the gaming community.	Tech	No	No	No	No
INKABites	Flash-fried Peruvian food truck fever franchise.	Food	No	No	No	No

The 10th Innovation & Entrepreneurship Teaching Excellence Awards

Sundafeast	Wholesale authentic Indonesian street food flavours.	Food	No	No	No	No
Night & Day	Sustainable workwear exchange marketplace for young professionals.	Fashion	No	No	No	No
Elm Park Restring	Racket collection, Restring & Return to clients.	Service	No	No	Yes	Yes

Author Biography

Pascal Loizeau, a seasoned entrepreneur in hospitality and retail, leveraged his Euro conversion consulting expertise to pivot into UK IT. Now, as Bath Student Enterprise's Project Coordinator, University of Bath, UK he ignites innovation by crafting educational experiences, plotting growth strategies, and nurturing the next generation of entrepreneurs.

Empowering Change: The Crowdfunding Learning Experience in Entrepreneurial Education

Daniel Michelis
Anhalt University of Applied Sciences, Germany
daniel.michelis@hs-anhalt.de

On the following pages, I describe how I have carried out various crowdfunding projects as part of an innovative course over the past few years in order to empower students to be more innovative and entrepreneurial with a very practical course. In this course, students embark on an adventurous journey through the world of crowdfunding, where they gain practical experience and develop skills in communication, project management and teamwork while supporting real-life social or environmental projects.

In this teaching format, students not only learn different skills, but they can also launch their own projects on crowdfunding platforms and turn their ideas into reality.

Figure 1: "Therapeutic riding - give children the joy of life!" (*Website-Link*)

The 10th Innovation & Entrepreneurship Teaching Excellence Awards

1. Introduction

Imagine walking into a seminar room at the beginning of the semester that has been transformed into a student command center from which students embark on an innovative learning journey into the unexplored educational field of crowdfunding. It is a transformative journey where they gain hands-on experience by working on real crowdfunding projects. Students will learn how to support social or environmental initiatives in the real world, developing essential skills in communication, project management and teamwork. Rather than just developing theoretical concepts, teams launch social or environmental initiatives for which they actively communicate with a wide range of people to gain their support. The aim is for students to rise above themselves and bring about real change through their projects.

2. Infrastructure

I have been carrying out crowdfunding projects such as those described in this article for around 10 years in the form of a learning expedition for the Master's degree course in Online Communication at Anhalt University of Applied Sciences. The starting point for this expedition is regular lectures that are enriched by exciting presentations by experts from leading crowdfunding platforms. These platform providers reveal the secrets of their systems to the students and prepare them for the challenges ahead.

Figure 2: Example from Introduction-Lecture: Donation Cycle

(Slide from *www.betterplace.org*)

After the introductory basics, the students choose a platform and set up their own project there, which is usually carried out in cooperation with a client from the field of social or ecological innovation.

This combination of applied basics and collaboration with innovative practice partners provides them with the necessary tools and knowledge, while giving them the freedom to make their own decisions and embark on their unusual learning journey.

3. General challenges and selected example projects

As with any real expedition, the students face a variety of challenges along their journey. First, they have to contact a real client and develop the upcoming project together. In doing so, they have to balance the requirements of the crowdfunding platform and the needs of the clients who want to raise funds for specific projects. In addition to organizational and communication challenges, legal and formal hurdles that arise when dealing with real funds must also be overcome. For example, many crowdfunding platforms only allow organizations that are classified as non-profit by the tax authorities. Handling the donations and dividing the projects into modules that appeal to donors in order to attract potential supporters pose further challenges.

Motivation within the teams often fluctuates, as described in detail below, especially when the initial euphoria wears off. However, like explorers navigating in opaque forests or uncharted seas, the teams find suitable solutions through experience, perseverance and creativity. Sometimes, however, individual discussions and support from lecturers and clients are needed to restore motivation and get the teams back on track. Over the past ten years, it has become clear that the major difficulties in particular have become valuable lessons on the students' journey of discovery.

To illustrate the teaching concept, selected projects are briefly described below.

Ecogon: A nature education board game

ECOGON is an innovative nature education game that teaches children, young people and adults about the environment and nature in a fun way. The idea for the game, for which almost 10,000 euros were raised on the crowdfunding platform EcoCrowd, came from a nature conservation student. Students from the Master's in Online Communication supported the nature conservation student in the conception and implementation of the crowdfunding campaign. This project illustrates how effectively students from different disciplines can work together and shows the power of interdisciplinary cooperation. Following successful crowdfunding, Ecogon was launched and the inventor has since developed further games (https://gaiagames.de/produkt/ecogon-english/). This project demonstrates not only the students' ability to secure funding, but also the lasting impact of their efforts as the game continues to educate players about biodiversity and ecosystems. (https://en.ecogon.de/project/crowdfunding/)

Reforestation for a sustainable world

In another project, students developed a campaign to finance a reforestation project. The aim of the project, which was carried out in collaboration with the startup Artenglück, is to raise €2,500 for the reforestation of a piece of forest in the Fläming Nature Park. The forest was destroyed by hurricane Kyrill and a bark beetle infestation and needs to be rebuilt.

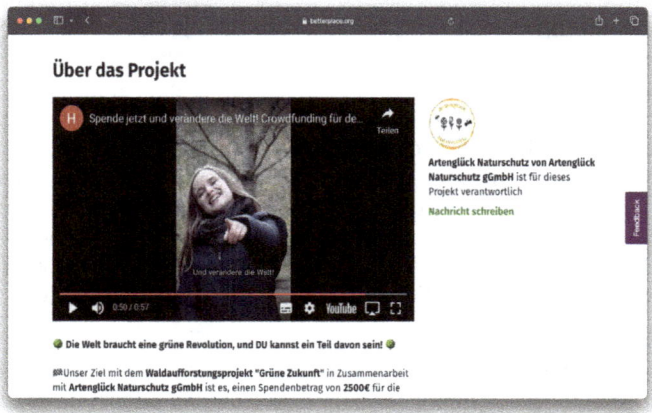

Figure 3: Project Video *https://youtu.be/WgAWrKS1Nrw?si=1DfiHY2ALmfhiLRi*

The special thing about this project is that the students even managed to push through internal resistance within the university and successfully financed the project. When the students tried to gain support for the project at a university event, they were refused permission. Despite this challenge, the students collectively decided to continue the project through other channels. They secured financial support from a company for which they had previously carried out a communication project. After presenting the results of this other communication project, the students successfully asked for crowdfunding support. The company agreed and subsequently even announced further direct support for the start-up, which was founded by a graduate. Following the successful financing, the reforestation, in which the students will then also participate, is planned for fall 2024. (www.betterplace.org/de/projects/128491-gruene-zukunft-waldaufforstung-fuer-eine-nachhaltige-welt)

School musical FLASHDANCE

This project aimed to realize a school musical by financing costumes, stage design and technical equipment. The students faced the challenge of mobilizing local communities and highlighting the cultural significance of the project. Their efforts paid off as they were able to secure enough funding to bring the musical to the stage and foster a sense of community involvement and support for the arts.

Daniel Michelis

Figure 4: Project Website Flashdance *https://www.startnext.com/herdermusicals*

Action Panda with WWF Deutschland

In the Action Panda project, students worked together with WWF Germany to combat plastic pollution in the oceans. They activated the local geocaching community and organized a so-called Cache-in, Trash-Out (CITO) event. This initiative involved community members collecting trash while geocaching and raised awareness for environmental protection. The aim was to collect one euro in donations for every meter that the community cleared the banks of the Saale River of garbage. The local press reported on the event, which attracted more supporters and spread the word about the project.

Figure 5: Project Website Cache and Collect
actionpanda.wwf.de/CacheAndCollect/idee

As the project grew, WWF Germany communicated the success via its newsletter, which even exceeded the funding target. This unexpected success required the students to quickly develop new communication measures and increase the fundraising target in the communication measures as well. The project not only exceeded the initial goals, but also demonstrated the students' ability to mobilize communities and manage dynamic project demands.

Figure 6: WWF Newsletter (Screenshot only in German)

Voice of Mother India

The "Voice of Mother India" project was carried out by a graduate as part of her master's thesis after she had successfully completed a crowdfunding project during her studies. This project aimed to empower and disseminate the voices of Indian women through a documentary series.

Figure 7: Students with local group
www.startnext.com/en/voiceofmotherindia

The campaign on Startnext was a great success and illustrated how effective crowdfunding can be as a tool to support social initiatives, even in the context of a thesis. The graduate was not only able to raise the necessary funds, but also received valuable support and recognition from the community, making the project a particular success.

Figure 8: "Voice of Mother India"
www.startnext.com/en/voiceofmotherindia

4. How students take up the teaching format

At the beginning of the semester, the projects initially seem like typical student seminar work. However, the students soon realize that the tasks are more unstructured and require a lot of self-organization. This realization often leads to disappointment and resistance, which often reduces motivation in the student teams after a short time. However, like entrepreneurs who, as innovators or entrepreneurs, face seemingly impossible obstacles, students must learn to reorient themselves and find their own way.

Through targeted one-on-one discussions, the lecturers can then usually pick up the mood again, and the collaboration with the clients increases acceptance and motivation. Despite other major challenges that arise during the implementation of the crowdfunding projects, the students ultimately understand the value of the projects for their learning process and personal growth. Almost exclusively positive feedback shows the ultimate acceptance and appreciation of the initiative.

5. Learning Experience and Results

The learning outcomes were recorded through written feedback from the students, but above all through feedback discussions in plenary, in groups and with the clients. These discussions enabled in-depth reflection and an exchange of experiences.

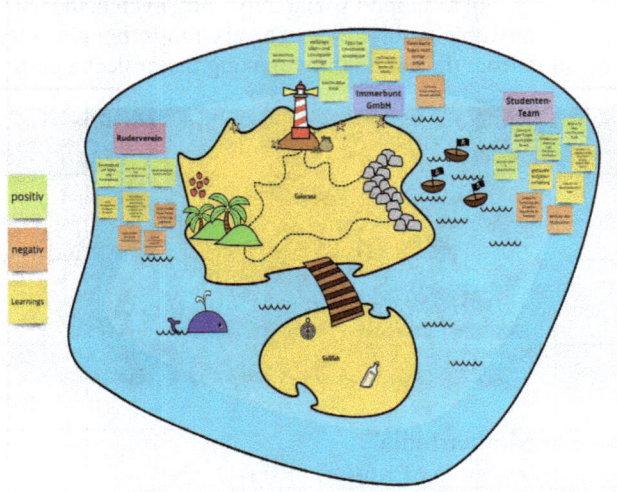

Figure 9: Exemplary retrospective with students and project partners

Figure 9 shows an exemplary visualization that was designed by a team of students for the feedback discussion at the end of the project. In addition to positive and negative feedback and the presentation of individual learnings, a picture of the mood during the course of the project was created, which is shown in figure 10.

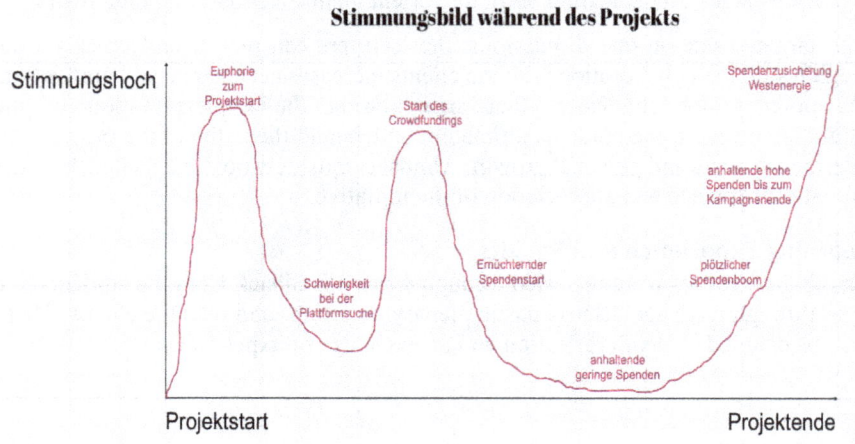

Figure 10: Example of the mood during the crowdfunding project (project feedback meeting)

Daniel Michelis

The mood curve shows the highs and lows that the students experienced during the course of the project:

1. Project start: At the start of the project, there is a neutral mood as the students familiarize themselves with the first steps and planning.
2. Euphoria at the start of the project: When active work on the project begins and the first ideas are developed, the mood rises sharply. The students are full of enthusiasm and euphoria as they can turn their visions into reality.
3. Difficulty in finding a platform: The first challenge arose when the students had difficulty finding a suitable crowdfunding platform. This led to a significant drop in morale as the uncertainty and complexity of the selection process had increased at this stage.
4. Crowdfunding launch: After overcoming the initial difficulties and selecting a platform, the mood rose again as crowdfunding officially started. The students were optimistic and excited about the next steps.
5. Disillusioning start to donations: The first few days of crowdfunding were disappointing as only a few donations were received. This led to a significant drop in sentiment and disappointment among the students.
6. Continued low donations: The period of low donations continued and sentiment remained low. Students had to deal with the frustration that their efforts were not immediately bearing fruit.
7. Sudden boom in donations: Unexpectedly, there was a sudden increase in donations (due to the change in communication from Instagram to LinkedIn). Students experienced a mood boost as their hard work finally showed results.
8. Sustained high donations until the end of the campaign: The positive trend continued and donations remained high until the end of the campaign. Spirits remained high as students see the goal getting closer and closer.
9. Donation pledge from partner company: Shortly before the end of the campaign, the students receive a large donation pledge from a local company. This led to a further increase in morale and a feeling of relief and satisfaction.
10. End of project: At the end of the project, the mood was at its peak as the funding target had been reached or even exceeded. The students felt successful and fulfilled.

A look at the mood curve shown allows us to derive some key findings. Learning through practical experience and emotional ups and downs appears to be effective. The mood curve also indicates that resilience is a crucial skill in entrepreneurship. Over the course of the project, students were able to experience how important it is to overcome setbacks and challenges and still remain motivated. This reflects the reality of entrepreneurship, where perseverance and adaptability are crucial to success. The emotional highs and lows also illustrate that theoretical knowledge should also be applied in practice in teaching. Through practical application, it becomes natural for students to adapt their communication strategies, project management skills and teamwork to real-life, often unpredictable situations. These practical experiences are a valuable addition to theoretical learning as they offer real challenges and a sense of achievement.

The mood curve also shows that feedback (also from the unknown donors) and the ability to adapt are crucial. By receiving direct feedback from donors, students were able to learn how the "market" responds to their own strategies and actions. This direct connection fosters an agile mindset, which has established itself as some important skills in today's fast-paced business world. Finally, student feedback exemplifies the importance of teamwork and networking. Students need to work together to find solutions and mobilize support, both within the team and through external partners. This fosters social skills and networks that are useful for future entrepreneurial activities.

Sometimes it also happens that a project is not successfully funded until the final donation amount is reached. In this case, the students then submit their feedback in the form of documentation and also share their feedback in writing, as the following feedback examples show:

> *"For me, the project was a complete success despite not reaching the donation target. We received a large number of small individual donations, which are still coming in bit by bit, which means that we have reached people with our project. I personally got a lot out of my first crowdfunding project."*

> *"I was able to take a lot away from this project. On the one hand, I was able to learn a lot about project management and teamwork. I was particularly pleased that we were able to collect many individual donations over the period and had interesting conversations with a wide variety of people who we were able to inspire for this project."*

> *"Many thanks for the exciting and challenging project! The collaboration with Artenglück was fabulous and the contact and support from Sophie really motivated us. Even though we weren't able to reach the desired donation target, we still got a lot out of this project and are keeping our fingers crossed for the future."*

6. Future Plans

As previous years have shown, the crowdfunding learning journey does not end with the successful funding of the projects. Future plans therefore include students continuing to support these projects after they have been funded and promoting awareness of such initiatives among the public. One example is the communicative support of a funded reforestation project, for which students will plant trees themselves in the fall of 2024 and document the campaign using multimedia. Through this ongoing involvement, we hope to spark new support and continue the cycle of learning and support. Previous graduates who have undertaken similar projects are now coming back as clients and strengthening the network between generations of students. This expansion of the crowdfunding learning journey allows us to keep exploring new horizons and creating lasting change.

7. Links and Sources

A selection of successful crowdfunding projects that students have realised in my courses in recent years. (Translated with DeepL)

- Reforestation for a sustainable world!
  https://www.betterplace.org/de/projects/128491-gruene-zukunft-waldaufforstung-fuer-eine-nachhaltige-welt
- Action Panda Crowdfunding with WWF Germany
  https://actionpanda.wwf.de/CacheAndCollect/idee
- School musical on a big stage: students use crowdfunding to support the Herder Musical Company in realising the school musical FLASHDANCE. realisation of the school musical FLASHDANCE.
  https://www.startnext.com/herdermusicals
- Use of crowdfunding to support the Leipzig clinic clowns n.e.V.
  https://www.betterplace.org/de/projects/50149-kranken-kindern-ein-lachen-schenken-leipziger-klinikclowns-n-e-v
- Flying elephants: Idea to make the stay easier for children at the University Medical Centre Hamburg-Eppendorf.
  https://www.betterplace.org/de/projects/46370-unterstutzt-kranke-kinder-im-malatelier-fliegende-elefanten
- Therapeutic horse riding: Students support the Deutsche Kinderkrebsnachsorge (German paediatric cancer aftercare) and campaign for therapeutic riding lessons for patients and their families. riding lessons for patients and their families. and their families.
  https://www.betterplace.org/de/projects/45012-therapeutisches-reiten-schenken-sie-kindern-lebensfreude
- Refugee Council Leipzig e.V.: Realisation of a crowdfunding for the support of young migrants in achieving the best possible educational qualification.
  https://www.betterplace.org/de/projects/31911-hilfe-nach-der-flucht-integration-durch-bildung-e-v
- ECOGON: Crowdfunding for an innovative nature education game that teaches knowledge and understanding about the environment and nature through play. https://www.ecocrowd.de/projekte/ecogon/
- Schoolchildren with language support needs: A crowdfunding project for the Rudolf Hildebrand School in Düsseldorf to support the purchase of reading pens. to support the purchase of reading pens.
  https://www.betterplace.org/de/projects/31831-unterstutzer-fur-schulkinder-mit-forderbedarf-sprache-in-dusseldorf-gesucht

- Blooming future: Saving 5000 m² of biodiversity!
  https://www.betterplace.org/de/projects/128831-bluehende-zukunft-5000-m-artenvielfalt-rettn

Author Biography

Daniel Michelis is a professor at Anhalt University of Applied Sciences, Germany where he teaches and researches how digital communication can contribute to the positive development of the economy and society. He works on social, economic and ecological challenges of economic and social transformation in a variety of projects.

Educating for Innovation – And on how Negative Responses to Innovation Abound

Manuel Au-Yong-Oliveira
INESC TEC, Porto, Portugal
GOVCOPP, DEGEIT, University of Aveiro, Aveiro, Portugal.
mao@ua.pt

Abstract: Innovation, one may think, is welcomed across the world. Not so. Innovative people have been persecuted throughout the ages – precisely for being innovative. Though the persecution often has had other labels. So, what do innovative people in organizational settings need to be aware of? What dangers do they face, including the jealousy of colleagues and bosses alike? Certain cases are discussed in class, and what could have been done differently in order for the innovation case to have been more successful. An innovative approach to innovation is adopted. Musicians and singers and song writers are given as examples as they are often recognizably innovative. Acting in groups or duos they also fall victim to what plagues innovators in organizational settings. What role may an innovation champion play? How might innovation be better managed? What pitfalls may be easily avoided by innovators? Humans are averse to change, of that there is no doubt, as the literature tells us. Albeit innovation involves and signifies change. Therefore, innovation will be resisted. History has important lessons for us, which we need to study. Students relate well to examples involving high profile individuals. Music provides for high comprehension levels on the subject of creativity and innovation. Learning about innovation can be fun. And writing an innovation plan while also focusing on technology and on digital transformation in itself is being innovative... How do students respond? With doubts and queries but also enthusiasm in an [academic] world where thinking outside the box is not genuinely/routinely encouraged...

Keywords: change, innovation, intellectual freedom, jealousy, fear

1. Introduction

The Management of innovation and technology course is part of the Master's in Management at the University of Aveiro. It is lectured once a week, in a three-hour slot, for the duration of the second semester (6 ECTS). The objectives of the course are to (from the course outline online here: https://www.ua.pt/en/uc/4379):

- "Sensitize students to the problems of innovation and technology as factors of productivity and increased competitiveness of organizations and companies.
- Familiarize students with concepts and definitions, processes and mechanisms, methodologies and techniques that allow their intervention and implementation of management practices and innovation control in organizations and companies.

- Analyse and discuss relevant national and international cases of innovative companies, organisations and regions, which allow the application of concepts related to: Organisational Innovation Management (technological or non-technological); Management of Sectoral, regional and national innovation systems.
- To enable students in the preparation of dissertations in the area of innovation management, through the domain of appropriate tools and techniques of scientific research in databases and management of bibliographical references."

The learning outcomes are (from the course outline online here: https://www.ua.pt/en/uc/4379):

- "To understand the issues linked to new business models and processes in the knowledge society.
- To be able to propose an innovation plan for the organisation or company where they are working.
- To be able to analyse trends in the evolution of business in the knowledge society."

What makes the course unique in its approach is that negative organisations are a main topic addressed. A negative organization may be defined as follows:

"A negative organisation is one where individual merit and innovation lose to the status quo and to the maintenance of the powerful relationships that govern the organisation." (Au-Yong-Oliveira, 2022, p.VII)

Can you imagine a firm (or nation) where individual interests supersede the organisation's (or nation's) best interests, as regards strategic development and what is best for the people and their futures? It may be more common than one at first suspects to have negative organisations (or negative nations) where the outcomes sought are not what common sense would tell us i.e., strategic development of the enterprise (with the stakeholders' best interests in mind).

Acemoglu and Robinson (2013) focused on *Why nations fail*. My lectures are a little different as they focus on smaller scale organisations. However, Acemoglu and Robinson (2013, p.3) are clear in that "when they reason about why a country such as Egypt is poor, most academics and commentators emphasize completely different factors" [such as]:

1. Geography [e.g., poor soils and climate];
2. Work ethic ["inimical to economic development"];
3. Cultural traits [bad for prosperity];
4. Beliefs ["inconsistent with economic success"];
5. Incorrect policies and strategies followed due to a lack of knowledge on the matter and to bad advisers.

Acemoglu and Robinson (2013, p.3) state however that: "The fact that Egypt has been ruled by narrow elites feathering their nests at the expense of society seems irrelevant... In this book we'll argue that the Egyptians in Tahrir Square, not most academics and commentators, have the right idea. In fact, Egypt is poor precisely because it has been ruled by a narrow elite that have organized society for their own benefit at the expense of the vast mass of people. Political power has been narrowly concentrated and has been used to create great wealth for those who possess it."

In organisations, in particular the civil service, and other subsidized firms, but not only there, the same conditions as mentioned for Egypt may be found, which leads to companies and organisations failing terribly over time, in relation to what they might have achieved, if they had followed the best strategies available to them. I refer to these types of organisations as negative organisations (or negative nations) and in such entities, as is to be expected, innovators who see a productive way forward will be expelled or terminated as they go against the interests of the *status quo* [the instituted power and hierarchy to be found at a given moment in time].

In Portugal, where we have a relationship-oriented culture (Solomon & Schell, 2009) which is also greatly averse to uncertainty and change (Hofstede, 2001) and hence to innovation (Au-Yong-Oliveira, 2022), the conditions and circumstances for negative organisations to exist and multiply are very significant. What other explanation may we find for the country having gone bankrupt three times in its recent democratic history and on its being subsidy-dependent (subsidies coming in from wealthier countries in the European Union) as we speak? Portugal has a number of young and promising graduates who are, in view of the existing powers-to-be and current organisational climates - dependent on relationships and on who you know and how you behave – seeking to emigrate in growing numbers to more meritocratic environments where countries and organisations really need and use innovation to survive and prosper in increasingly competitive economies.

Hence the emphasis for my students and during my lectures is to not overtly show one's prowess and competence for fear of being terminated for posing a threat to the *status quo* and instead to certainly disguise as much as possible that they are innovative and only show their "true colours" when necessary and to their advantage.

Jealousy from colleagues and bosses is also a subject of discussion (Walter & Au-Yong-Oliveira, 2022) and real-life examples to this end are given in class.

2. The infrastructure

In select lectures I will play music by famous musicians. For this I will need a video projector, a good wi-fi connection, and loud-speakers – all of which I have access to. Students, despite being from later generations, relate well to songs sung by the duo Simon and Garfunkel. As is known, the duo did not last beyond its initial fame and broke up during its peak. One reason for this is the jealousy felt between the members of the duo (Stanton, 2024) in particular the fame and recognition Art Garfunkel was getting for singing songs (with his angelical and unique voice) written by Paul Simon (e.g., the song "Bridge over trouble water"). This was incomprehensible to Paul Simon who ended the relationship which had started while they were still in school – Garfunkel having protected Simon from boys bullying him at an early age and due to obvious physical differences (Garfunkel very tall and Simon of lesser stature).

Stanton (2024) wrote that: "We had an uneven partnership because I was writing all of the songs and basically running the sessions," Simon said in the documentary. "Artie'd be in the control room… he'd say, 'Yeah, that's good,' but it was an uneven balance of power... Simon also admitted to a certain amount of jealousy over Garfunkel's singing abilities, particularly when they performed "Bridge Over Troubled Water" live. Simon recalled it would earn a standing ovation and he'd be jealous, thinking, "I wrote that song."." Please see image 1.

Image 1: A tale of the song which ended the Simon & Garfunkel duo is told in class – human relations and innovation go hand-in-hand

Another exercise demonstrative of how relationships are so important to innovation and other organizational outcomes is the playing of the opening scene of *The Godfather*. By Mario Puzo. Please see image 2. In it one may see how a law-abiding citizen becomes a part of the Godfather's network (owing him a favour to be collected in the future) due to a request made of the Godfather (initially the request was to kill for money – but relationship cultures are more about favours owed than transactions for money).

Manuel Au-Yong-Oliveira

Opening Scene Godfather

Image 2: A story on how Portugal's Latin and Southern European culture is not far away from the culture described in *The Godfather* – the emphasis is on relationships and networks

3. The challenges

Some students will perhaps question how [negative] organisations (and society) will react badly to innovators. How they may be expelled and terminated for showing promising ways forward and for innovating, generally. However, they will eventually get to understand what I am saying and even become "evangelists" of the theme beyond the lecture theatre and within their circles (of friends and acquaintances).

Therefore, some answers follow to the questions posed above:

What role may an innovation champion play?

Firms should appoint internal innovation champions as "the toughest sales job for anyone is to sell their own company on new ideas and new opportunities." (Howell, 2005, p.108). Take the Nokia case, where the dumbphone triumphed over the smartphone, due to the sheer significance (unit sales and profit) and power of that division – having pushed the new smartphone inventors to the sidelines.

> *"To overcome organizational inertia or fierce opposition and move new product ideas from small to large project endeavors, market launch, and ultimate market success requires champions... effective champions differ from ineffective ones in their personal characteristics and behaviors... Effective*

The 10th Innovation & Entrepreneurship Teaching Excellence Awards champions are distinguished by three behaviors: conveying confidence and enthusiasm about the innovation; enlisting the support and involvement of key stakeholders; and persisting in the face of adversity." (Howell, 2005, p.108).

During my career in industry, I did not come across a formal innovation champion role, as described by Howell (2005), at the companies where I worked - nor at the companies we had exchanges and partnerships with. While with Worthington Cylinders Europe (and stationed in Portugal) I was informally charged with the role of innovation champion (by an internal but international consultant I was doing work for, from the USA, to make the company turnaround a success) and my job was to think positively and get people to adopt and adapt to the changes we were implementing. However, this was quite far from my formal roles – in training and marketing. Later, as a researcher, I came across CIOs – Chief Innovation Officers – including in Portugal; but their role was different and quite a solitary one, far from the corridors of power.

How might innovation be better managed?

Innovation might be better managed by better managing envy. Envy regarding those who are better at innovation. There could be a new role in organisations (for example, in the Human Resource department) called the "Envy Director". Walter and Au-Yong-Oliveira (2022, p.1) "suggest that envy not only has a direct positive influence on alignment with negative boss behaviors and ostracism, but also an indirect influence on ostracism mediated by alignment with negative boss behaviors. Another important result of the present investigation refers to the negative effect of envy on the predisposition to innovative behavior. The results suggest that the greater the envy, the lower the innovative behavior."

What pitfalls may be easily avoided by innovators?

By being aware of resistance to change and innovation and of envy, innovators may be more prepared for barriers and other attacks on their work. Innovators may be under the naïve impression that as they have talent that colleagues and organisations will automatically help them in their endeavours. Nothing could be further from the truth. By being innovative this will attract envy and all sorts of problems with the *status quo* – the existing state of things, the existing hierarchy.

Humans are averse to change, of that there is no doubt, as the literature tells us. Albeit innovation involves and signifies change. Therefore, innovation will be resisted.

Product innovation may very well mean that "in comes the new and out goes the old". This in turn may mean that existing expertise and people linked to the old product line will be surpassed by new expertise held by new people. Whether the existing people and knowledgeable about the old product will be invited to be a part of the new team will remain to be seen. They may not even be capable of catching up with the new technology, in an effective, efficient, and timely manner. Hence, humans may have good reason to be afraid of change and of innovation as it may alter how they live and earn money. Albeit change and innovation may come from inside the organization or be forced on us by a competitor – signifying that in a competitive market environment facing and adapting to change and innovation is not an option but rather a question of survival. To remain competitive organisations must be positive and promote meritocracies and a "survival of the fittest environment". Competence and not relationships should be the basis of promotions and advancement. This is difficult in more loyalty-rewarding and loyalty-seeking environments – such as those found in Southern Europe.

Using the words of a friend and senior executive who has read one of my books on negative organisations and competitiveness (Graça & Au-Yong-Oliveira, 2024), there are a lot of negative organisations to be found in the marketplace. Albeit schools and universities practically do not touch on the subject, he stated. The negativity is brought on by people and as a result of their insecurities and vulnerabilities and by an inability to deal with other people. Given the importance of communication and of needing to deal with colleagues in a work environment (where one will spend most of the day, at work...) this should be a focus at school. Therefore, the basis of all these problems is a shortcoming of the academic environment – from high school right through the different levels of higher education (and including vocational education and training [VET] too).

4. How the initiative was received

Numerous students have contacted the author/teacher Manuel regarding his novel and different teaching methods. One student said in an e-mail: "Dear Teacher, Thank you very much in advance for your support and your commitment to the students. The teaching method used in your curricular units is innovative, engaging and fruitful, which also motivated us to do this task [assignment]. We were delighted [...] All the best."

5. The learning outcomes

The outcomes were evaluated via the internal University of Aveiro quality channels and system. Large scale responses were gathered from students who anonymously and voluntarily rate the lecturer and his performance on a number of items. The results from the academic year 2022-2023 follow in the images captured. The TTG group of 8.03 indicates a level of overall performance of "Best Practice" level at the University of Aveiro (score of equal to or above 8.0 and from a scale of 1.0 to 9.0). Please see image 3.

The 10th Innovation & Entrepreneurship Teaching Excellence Awards

pedagogical student survey
report on a course unit
and a teacher

2nd Semester | 2022-23

unit	curricular	unit	UnivResp	no. resp	% resp
degeit	47613	INNOVATION AND TECHNOLOGY MANAGEMENT	70	17	24.29%

teacher

unit	uu	name of lecturer	edoc	no. resp	% resp
degeit	mao@ua.pt	MANUEL LUÍS AU-YONG OLIVEIRA	68	17	25.00%

subtitle
UnivResp - universe of students responding to the pedagogical survey nº
edoc - number of students associated with the teacher in the classes
nº resp - number of students who responded to the survey
% resp - percentage of responses

characterisation of the teacher

tab.1

perg	n1	n2	n3	n4	n5	n6	n7	n8	n9	so/na	total	valid	md	average	Sx
P18	0	0	1	0	1	1	3	6	5	0	17	17	8	7.53	1.62
P19	0	1	0	1	1	1	3	2	8	0	17	17	8	7.41	2.09
P20	0	0	0	0	0	1	4	4	7	1	17	16	8	8.06	1.00
P21	0	0	0	1	1	0	6	2	5	2	17	15	7	7.47	1.51
P22	0	0	0	0	0	0	1	6	9	1	17	16	9	8.50	0.63
P23	0	1	0	0	1	0	4	5	4	2	17	15	8	7.40	1.84
P24	0	0	0	0	0	0	2	4	10	1	17	16	9	8.50	0.73
P25	0	0	0	0	0	0	1	5	9	2	17	15	9	8.53	0.64
P26	0	0	0	0	0	2	4	4	7	0	17	17	8	7.94	1.09
P27	0	0	0	0	1	0	0	7	9	0	17	17	9	8.35	1.00
P28	0	0	0	0	0	0	1	4	12	0	17	17	9	8.65	0.61
TTG	0	2	1	2	5	5	29	49	85	9	187	178	8	8.03	1.32
P29	0	0	0	1	0	0	6	5	5	0	17	17	8	7.71	1.26

subtitle

P18 Capacity to stimulate and motivate students for the course unit
P19 Creating a climate favourable to learning and the active participation of students
P20 Stimulating student autonomy
P21 Monitoring student work
P22 Knowledge of programme content
P23 Organisation of content and activities during contact hours
P24 Teacher punctuality
P25 Availability of assistance to students
P26 Clarity of presentation
P27 Teacher relationship with the student
P28 Compliance with assessment rules agreed with students
TTG Group Totals (P18-P28)
Q29 Global evaluation of teacher performance

n1..n9 No. of answers to option 1 ... no. of answers to option 9 (scale of 1 to 9)
so/na No opinion/Not applicable
valid No. of valid answers (without "so/na")
md Sx Median - 50th percentile
Standard Deviation (measure of dispersion of values around their mean)

Image 3: The classification given to the lecturer of the Management of Innovation and Technology – year 2022-2023 – at "Best Practice" level for the University of Aveiro

6. Plans to further develop the initiative

Another book coauthored by the candidate has come out, in August 2024 (Graça & Au-Yong-Oliveira, 2024). The publisher is the prestigious Springer Nature firm and the title of the book is as follows: *Competitiveness strategies for Negative Organizations: Challenging the Status Quo*. Please see images 4 and 5.

Image 4: A book coauthored by the candidate offering solutions to negative firms

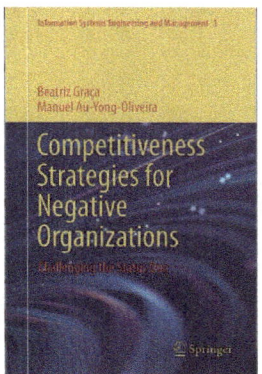

Image 5: The cover of the candidate's most recent book - coauthored - on negative organisations

This book has additional important lessons to be passed on to students – lessons on what a negative organisation is and lessons on how to overcome them and prevail – individually and as an organization.

A book of exercises and on positive organizations is also to be published, up and beyond this recent article by the candidate on "Transformational leadership and positive organisations - feeding the debate with autoethnography" (Au-Yong-Oliveira, 2023).

Hence the discussion is not only focused on the negative but on the positive, also. Positive aspects of the life in organisations tend to stick more with students, offering more hope, albeit the use of portraying the "truth" and different scenarios on innovation are seen to be worthwhile and of value to society and higher education students and scholars alike.

Additional reading is also to be undertaken, of such books as (Edmondson, 2018):

The fearless organization: Creating Psychological Safety in the Workplace for Learning, Innovation, and Growth. Please see image 6.

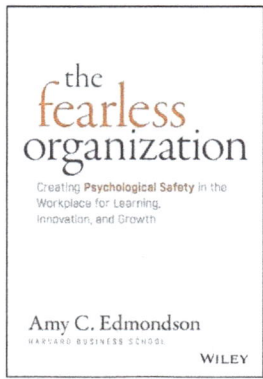

Image 6: If authors are writing about the fearless organization it is because there is reason to have fear [felt by innovators and other competent people in organizations]

From the description on Amazon.co.uk one may read that:

> *"The Fearless Organization: Creating Psychological Safety in the Workplace for Learning, Innovation, and Growth offers practical guidance for teams and organizations who are serious about success in the modern economy. With so much riding on innovation, creativity, and spark, it is essential to attract and retain quality talent—but what good does this talent do if no one is able to speak their mind?"*

And that is what my lectures are about – on the decision to speak one's mind or not. On the decision regarding choosing to survive, or not, as individuals and organisations. As organisations are dangerous places – especially for the innovative and competent individual.

7. Concluding remarks

I hence aim to end the perspective of the individual who naively thinks that being of use to society, by being creative and innovative, is a story that will always have a happy ending. By being aware of different types of organization – both "positive" (rewarding of innovative individuals in a meritocratic environment) and "negative" (where powerful self-serving individuals exist to superimpose their own strategies on organisations, to "feather their own nest") – I foresee that more chances for Portugal to change will exist and that, hopefully, less young graduates will see a need to emigrate. In an aging and overly subsidized country, Portugal is in desperate need of change and of higher education courses showing how that change may occur – with the proper tools in place and while properly planning for change. We need to have the entrepreneurial spirit alive and spreading – and soft skills and transversal skills are indeed important to survive organizational politics and to become important decision-makers who are not afraid of innovation and of the best strategy to move forward, for all the stakeholders involved. Image 7 shows a recent headline from the media (Donn, 2024) on Portuguese youth emigration levels. Which are alarming and need to be curbed. For our nation to have a future. With less negative organisations and more meritocratic environments.

Image 7 Almost a third of Portuguese women of 'fertile age' live abroad

Donn (2024) goes on to state that: "Almost 30% of young people born in Portugal live outside the country. More than 850,000 young Portuguese (between the ages of 15-39) have left the country and currently live abroad – almost a third of them being 'women of a fertile age'. The exodus will have a "brutal effect on national fertility and the labour market", warn experts. These are salient points coming out of the **"Atlas of Portuguese Emigration"**, compiled and ready to be presented next week by the Observatory of Migrations. What it boils down to is that **Portugal has the highest level of emigration in Europe**, and **one of the highest in the world**, says *Expresso*, running the story as its broadsheet edition cover story this week."

We hope that the objective of the course Management of innovation and technology, at the University of Aveiro, has been understood, in a country desperately needing innovation and innovative individuals [to stay in the country and in Portuguese organisations]. For the country to prosper and grow we will need positive, meritocratic organisations rather than negative organisations where existing relationships and loyalties dictate strategy. Sound economic principles and globally accepted strategic notions are necessary and need to be adhered to for sustained success in competitive markets.

Acknowledgements

This work was financially supported by the Research Unit on Governance, Competitiveness and Public Policies (UIDB/04058/2020) + (UIDP/04058/2020), funded by national funds through FCT - Fundação para a Ciência e a Tecnologia.

References

Acemoglu, D., Robinson, J.A. (2013). *Why nations fail. The origins of power, prosperity and poverty*. Profile Books, London.

Au-Yong-Oliveira, M. (2022). *Negative organisations and how to overcome them. Fighting to promote innovation and change*. Faro: Sílabas & Desafios.

Au-Yong-Oliveira, M. (2023). A liderança transformacional e as organizações positivas - alimentando o debate com a autoetnografia [Transformational leadership and positive organisations - feeding the debate with autoethnography]. ICIEMC 2023 Proceedings, Nº4.

Donn, N. (2024). 30% of young people born in Portugal live outside the country. *Portugal Resident*. 12-01-2024. Available here: https://www.portugalresident.com/30-of-young-people-born-in-portugal-live-outside-country/, accessed on 10-06-2024.

Edmondson, A.C. (2018). *The fearless organization: Creating Psychological Safety in the Workplace for Learning, Innovation, and Growth*. Wiley.

Graça, B., Au-Yong-Oliveira, M. (2024). *Competitiveness strategies for negative organisations – Challenging the Status Quo*. Switzerland: Springer.

Hofstede, G. (2001). *Culture's Consequences: Comparing Values, Behaviors, Institutions and Organizations Across Nations*. Thousand Oaks: Sage Publications.

Howell, J.M. (2005). The right stuff: identifying and developing effective champions of innovation. *Academy of Management Executive*, 19(2), pp.108-119.

Solomon, C.M., Schell, M.S. (2009). *Managing across cultures – The seven keys to doing business with a global mindset*. USA: McGraw-Hill.

Stanton, E. (2024). Paul Simon's friendship with Art Garfunkel destroyed by jealousy, 'uneven partnership'. Fox News. Available at: https://www.foxnews.com/entertainment/paul-simons-friendship-art-garfunkel-destroyed-jealousy-uneven-partnership, accessed on 10-06-2024.

Walter, C.E., Au-Yong-Oliveira, M. (2022). An exploratory study on the barriers to innovative behavior: the spiteful effect of envy. *Journal of Organizational Change Management*. DOI 10.1108/JOCM-02-2022-0034.

Author Biography

Manuel Au-Yong-Oliviera is an Associate Professor with Habilitation at the University of Aveiro where he has been lecturing since 2009. In 2023 Manuel received an honorable mention in the annual research awards at the University of Aveiro for his work in the social sciences. Manuel lectures on strategy, innovation and technology, and marketing.

Democratizing Entrepreneurship and Innovation Education Through "No-Code" AI Platforms

Leif Sundberg and Jonny Holmström
Swedish Center for Digital Innovation (SCDI),
Department of Informatics, Umeå University, Sweden.
leif.sundberg@umu.se
jonny.holmstrom@umu.se

Abstract: With the rapid development of artificial intelligence (AI) systems, such as machine learning (ML), it is certain that students will encounter and use these technologies in their professional careers. However, as ML technologies are commonly associated with technical professions, such as computer science and engineering, incorporating training in their use into non-technical educational programs is challenging. Thus, there is a need for approaches that integrate AI and ML technologies in educational programs in social sciences. To do so, we present a teaching initiative where "no-code" AI platforms are used in higher education. The initiative's core objective is to democratize AI and make it accessible to students across various disciplines, enabling them to use ML tools for entrepreneurial and innovative purposes, without the need for extensive programming knowledge. In this chapter, we present challenges and opportunities in using no-code AI in a case-based teaching setting where students receive hands-on experience in using ML to create business value.

1. Introduction

With the rapid development of artificial intelligence (AI), it is certain that students will encounter and use such technologies in their professional careers. However, technologies such as machine learning (ML) are often associated with technical professions (e.g., STEM), and training in their use in social science programs is challenging. This gap hampers multidisciplinary approaches to developing AI both in education and practice. As noted by Ma and Siau (2019, p. 1), "Higher education needs to change and evolve quickly and continuously to prepare students for the upheavals in the job market caused by AI, ML, and automation." However, despite abundant research on applications of AI in educational settings (e.g., Luan and Tsai, 2021; Humble and Mozelius, 2022), less attention has been paid to instructing students with non-technical backgrounds in AI/ML's practical use (Kayhan, 2022).

This chapter outlines a teaching initiative led by Associate Professor Leif Sundberg and Professor Jonny Holmström at the Department of Informatics, Umeå University, Sweden, which addresses this gap by integrating "no-code" AI platforms into the curriculum. These platforms are easy to use with little to no installation requirements (as they are cloud-based) and have graphical interfaces that help users train ML models (Sundberg and Holmström, 2023; Geske et al., 2021; Lins et al., 2021). Examples of no-code AI platforms include BigML, Google AutoML, Teachable Machine, and RoboFlow.

The initiative's core objective is to democratize AI and make it accessible to students across various disciplines, enabling them to use ML tools for entrepreneurial and innovative purposes without the need for extensive programming knowledge. In the following sections, we outline how we integrate the use of no-code AI in a module in a master course titled 'AI for business' (15 credits), to give the students hands-on experience in training ML models by engaging in a case-based task, using a principle of instruction approach (Merrill, 2012).

The course module has been running for three consecutive years, 2021-2023. As the students come from different educational backgrounds, we do not include in-depth examinations of phenomena such as neural networks and instead focus on providing students with information to get hands-on experience in training ML models to create business value.

The course module is initiated with an overview lecture on the current status of ML, and includes descriptions of how increases in the scale of datasets, together with improvements in algorithms and processing speed have increased capabilities for machines to 'learn'. The lecture includes a presentation of the fundamentals of the ML workflow (Figure 1), the importance of data work, and challenges organizations that want to leverage value from ML face.

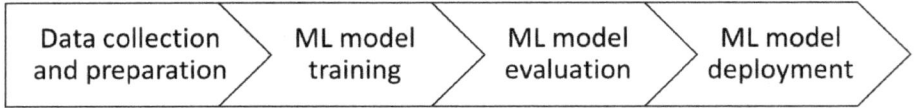

Figure 1: A simplified ML workflow

An important part of the lecture involves outlining the kinds of problems that can be solved by using ML. As noted by Kayhan (2022, p. 123), "many students lack the preparation for the workforce because they cannot conceptualize valid input-output relationships for the problems they propose to solve using ML". Thus, despite the widespread hype surrounding intelligent systems, there is a lack of specificity regarding the kinds of problems algorithms can help organizations solve (such as classifications and anomaly detection).

Then, we turn our attention to demonstrating the functionality of the no-code AI platform. Here, free datasets from Kaggle can be used to demonstrate how ML models can be trained on tabular data, images, and text. One example we displayed is to use images of moon craters to build a model capable of identifying potholes in roads (see, Figures 2 and 3).

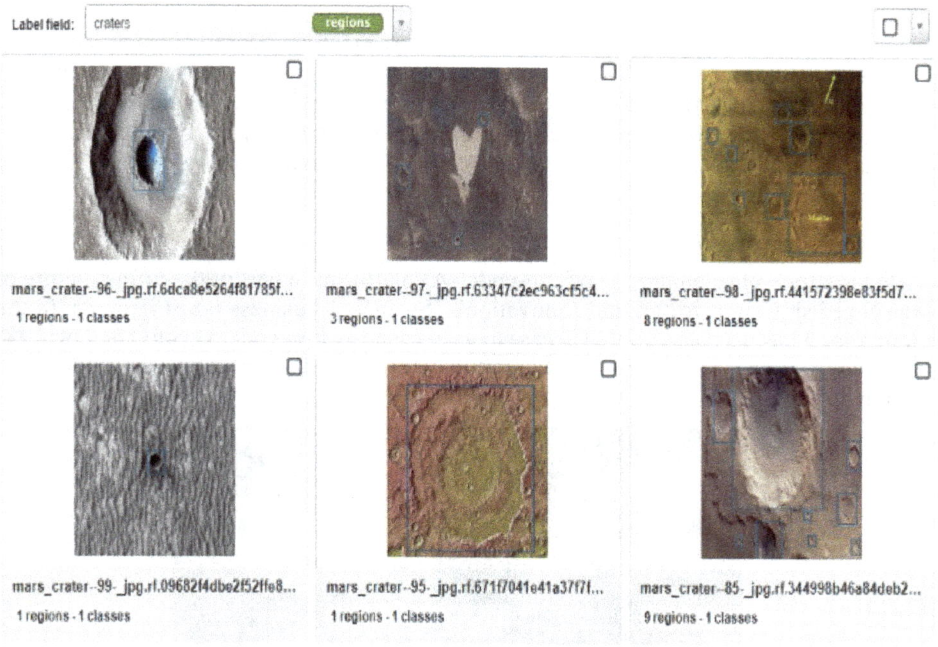

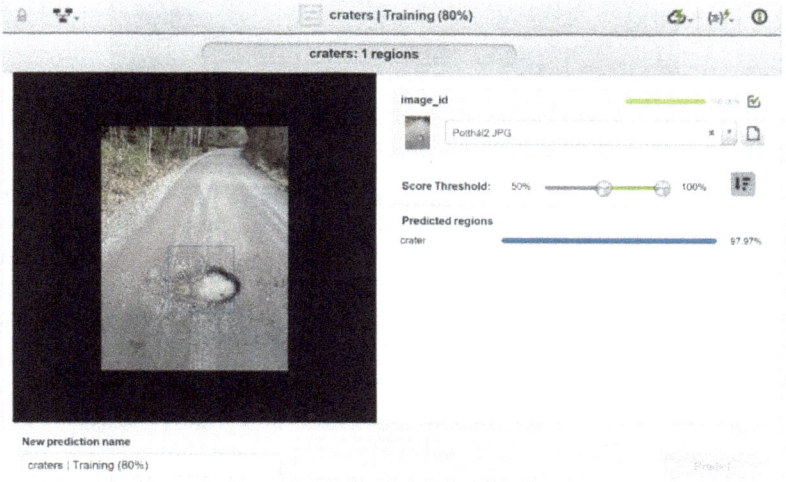

Figure 2. Example of image annotation in the BigML Platform

Figure 3. A model trained on crater data identifies a pothole.

We end the demonstration by explaining the procedure of evaluating ML models, including common issues like data bias and overfitting. Here, receiver operating characteristic (ROC) curves and confusion matrices were used to aid students' understanding of ML outputs and the need for cautious deployment due to the probabilistic nature of these models. We used examples like spam filters and medical diagnostics to illustrate the trade-offs between common measures like recall and precision.

2. The infrastructure

The initiative relies on the use of "no-code" AI platforms, a part of the infrastructure of the Swedish Center for Digital Innovation's (SCDI) AI business lab (Figure 4). In the long run, it has been argued that access to user-friendly, low-code AI could democratize the adoption of these systems and stimulate their multidisciplinary use (Sundberg & Holmström. 2023).

Figure 4: The SCDI AI Business lab at the Department of Informatics, Umeå University

The course module has been running for three consecutive years, with different cases. In the first year, a fictive case from the welding industry was used. This case is described in more detail in Sundberg and Holmström (2022) and Sundberg and Holmström (2024a). In the second year, a real case in collaboration with a welding firm was used. The third year included a case in the insurance industry and included building a chatbot using ChatGPT in addition to using no-code AI. See Appendix A for a summarization of the case narratives used in 2021-2023.

When the case is introduced, the students are divided into groups and assigned the task of helping an organization use ML to solve a problem. The example below was used in 2021 when the students were tasked to help a welding firm, "WeldCorp" to use ML as an instrument to assess the quality of their welding joints. First, we provide a backstory of the organization. Then, the students are given instructions for developing a ML solution:

> Your assignment is to help WeldCorp sustain its growth by leveraging machine learning. Specifically, your task is to analyze welding images (images of good and bad welding points) to develop a model – using the no-code AI platform – that can be useful for WeldCorp in a quality assurance context.
> - Describe and justify your choices regarding the data processing, problem selection, and model training in the no-code AI platform.
> - Describe how you evaluated your model's predictions. Are they accurate enough to use live for WeldCorp? Why/why not?
> - Discuss: What could be done by WeldCorp to improve the model's results? How would they implement this type of solution in their business?

An important aim of this assignment is to prompt students to think about and justify their choices during training, and the output of their model(s), rather than simply striving to optimize the performance of the model(s). As the module is part of an AI *business* course, we want the students to emphasize how organizations can generate value with ML.

The students are then given access to a no-code AI platform. Midway through the course module, a Q&A session is held with the student groups. Typically, most questions from the students concern data requirements (amount required, formats, and tentative workarounds). This is consistent with expectations as data collection and processing play a key role in ML and "there is no AI without data" (Gröger, 2021).

Between the Q&A and final seminar, the students receive supervision, and we can observe their progression in the no-code AI platform as they collect and label data and apply the procedures previously demonstrated to them to train and iteratively evaluate models.

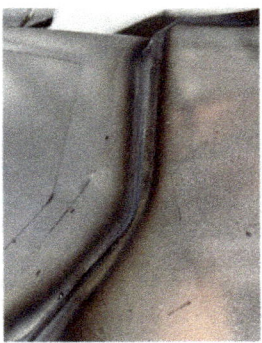 

Figure 5: Example of images collected by the students in 2022. The left image illustrates a clean ("good") welding joint while the right contains unwanted "spatter" around the joint.

The final seminar revolves around written reports and oral presentations by the student groups. During discussions the students are encouraged to reflect upon the ML process, to enable them to integrate their acquired skills. Thus, in addition to discussing the ML workflow, the students also propose ideas for operationalizing their work in a live setting, such as using automated cameras to feed data on welding points for evaluation by the ML model. In this seminar, the teachers mainly play a facilitating role, as the students pose questions and reflect on their results and learning.

3. The challenges

Implementing this novel teaching approach presents several challenges related to live-case proposals, data access, and the black-boxed nature of ML. These challenges are addressed through a supportive learning environment that fosters curiosity and experimentation, rather than algorithmic optimization. Students often initially face challenges related to understanding the ML workflow and the importance of data quality. Overcoming these obstacles involves structured workshops, hands-on sessions with the no-code platform as described above, and continuous feedback throughout the course. Our approach specifically entails two challenges, outlined below.

First, *the experimental nature of ML*. It is important to formulate a live case that is feasible to solve with ML. Finding an appropriate case may be time-consuming and it can be difficult to assess the case before tests have been conducted on a sample of data. In Figure 6, one of the teachers is doing data collection at a local welding company to create such a sample. This brings a degree of uncertainty into the teaching process, which is both daunting and exciting, but data repositories, such as Kaggle, can provide a backup plan.

Figure 6: Data collection at a local welding firm.

Second, *AI platform issues*. Different platforms have different functions and capabilities. Some focus more on textual data, while others are more suitable for visual recognition tasks. They also vary when it comes to maturity regarding user management, which may cause issues when students are to be divided into groups. Often these issues can be sorted out with proper planning, but sometimes there is a need for assistance from the platform provider. Meanwhile, the platform market is rapidly evolving. The platform we used during year one (Peltarion) was disbanded when the company behind it was acquired. Thus, it became necessary to rapidly procure a new platform (BigML). Here, it is also important to inform students to not upload sensitive data, depending on the regulatory context of the educational setting (e.g., GDPR), and the cloud provider used for data storage. A related challenge is the rapid evolution of AI. With the advent of generative AI and ChatGPT, in 2023 we deemed it necessary to introduce such tools in the course, and we did so by adding a task to create instructions (a prompt) for a chatbot that could assess car damage for an insurance company (see, Figure 7). Thus, it is necessary to secure time during course planning every year, to account for AI-specific issues.

TestStud2023

Hello, I'm sorry to hear about your car. Please provide one or several photos of the damage to your car so I can analyze it for you.

Thank you for the photo. I will analyze the damage.

The image shows significant damage to the front left side of the car, including a broken headlamp and a dented bumper and hood. This appears to be a severe type of damage.

Please provide the following details:

1. Time, date, and address where the damage occurred.

Figure 7: Example of a student case where ChatGPT is used to analyze car damage for an insurance company.

4. How the initiative was received by the users or participants

An important part of the mentioned principles of instruction teaching framework is the notion of "reflection" as learners continuously reflect on their learning. In our live cases, we encourage reflections as an integrated part of both the end seminar and formal course evaluations. We aim to educate "reflective practitioners" (Schön, 2017) who engage in reflection during their practices to improve their understanding and performance. Reflection includes being aware of your actions and their effects, both during and after activities, to allow for adjustment and improvements to inform future practice. This is especially important in settings where tacit knowledge is important, and complex, uncertain, and unique situations (e.g., ML development), to build learning cultures in e.g., organizations. Our students often highlight how they appreciate the use of live cases in combination with the opportunity to work close to technology, to iteratively build solutions, and to consider the impact of applying such solutions in organizational settings. The course module has received enthusiastic feedback from students and faculty alike, as illustrated by the following quote from a student:

> "For me, the barrier to understanding the practical use of AI (or to ever try it myself) has been my lack of programming and coding skills. With the no-code approach, I got the opportunity to try experiments and thus got a 'black-boxed' grasp of how it works. With that, I could focus on the problem that I wanted to solve, the learning dataset and its effect on the results, and also on the result itself. So, I think I learned more about AI in this course than I have in all the other courses combined, and that is without any code."

The above quote stems from our qualitative course evaluation, which consists of the following items:

> Background variables: Educational background | Age | Gender.
>
> Questions:
>
> Describe if / how your previous education has aided you during the course.
>
> Did the use of the "no-code" machine learning platform contribute to your learning of AI? If so, how? If not, why not?
>
> What have you learned about the role of data when training machine learning models during the course?
>
> Supervised ML requires data labeling. Data labeling occurs in a social context where actors label the images. As a result, there may be disagreement between actors. How do you deal with such disagreements in ML contexts?

The above questions are specifically targeted to the course module to ensure we receive feedback on how the students perceive how both the use of no-code AI and the data work it entails contribute to their learning. In the feedback, the students heavily emphasized an increase in their awareness of the importance of data, and how the no-code approach enabled them to focus on important features of the datasets used, potential flaws in them, and problem-solving rather than model-optimization, as illustrated by the following quotations:

> "I've obtained practical knowledge and experience of the impact of data. And I've seen the impact of flaws in the dataset first-hand. Thus, I think this was an optimal learning method considering our (and my) educational background."
>
> "[I've learnt] that data matters! The choice, generating and cleansing of data are crucial."

Meanwhile, the initiative has not only enhanced students' AI literacy and entrepreneurial mindset but also contributed to an overall interest in AI at the department. Here, we have achieved synergy effects with related projects to explore the integration of deep tech into higher education. Finally, we cannot underscore enough the importance of the course in democratizing AI, by making it accessible to a wide audience of students from different educational backgrounds.

5. The learning outcomes

In line with the course curriculum (Umeå University, 2024), the learning objectives of the exercise were to "Account for and explain the role of AI in organizational value creation", by giving the students first-hand experience of training ML models.

The assignments associated with the live cases typically revolve around three questions (see, Appendix B for a more detailed description of the assignments):

First, the students need to motivate their choices made during the data collection, processing, and model training in the platform. The purpose of this question is to highlight how the outcomes of ML systems are heavily dependent on human choices during their development.

Second, the students should reflect on the evaluations they made of the trained models' performance. Are they good enough to use in operational settings? The purpose of this question is to ensure students are familiar with how ML systems output probabilities rather than certainties, and that there are different ways to assess these outputs.

Third, the students need to describe how the organization at hand can implement the ML models in their daily operations. This question is crucial as the step from training a model to deploying it in an organization is vast and requires strategic considerations and changes in current processes.

The students are expected to present the results in the form of a short paper (max 10 pages) and orally at the final seminar. The report and seminar are graded as pass or fail. The criteria used for evaluation are related to a) having presented a logically coherent suggestion for the case, both in writing and orally during the seminar, and b) formulating results and associated discussion in a grammatically correct way and with consistent use of concepts and terms. These assignments are accompanied by a battery of individual questions for the whole course.

Our teaching methods, combined with informal and formal evaluations ensure that we a) use live cases for practical impact, and b) translate theoretical knowledge to practical skills. These outcomes are described in more detail below.

Practical impact. We invite representatives from the case organization to attend the final seminar. The aim is both to connect our students with potential future employers, but also to set the stage for a practical contribution of the teaching cases, and inspire these representatives to explore the opportunities provided by ML. We see great synergies between research activities in the AI lab and our teaching, as the live cases contribute to expanding our industry networks and set the stage for a range of activities. Examples include deepened student engagements with the organizations from the live cases (e.g., during master theses), and joint research funding applications with these organizations.

Translating theoretical knowledge to practical skills. Another outcome is the practical application of theoretical knowledge. It is important to note that although the students are acquiring practical skills in applying ML, the teaching activities are heavily rooted in theoretical papers on the use of ML in organizations from top journals in the information systems field. Exemplary papers from this literature we use in the course cover crucial aspects of ML development, such as the importance of including domain experts (van den Broek et al., 2021), uncertainties during data labeling (Lebovitz et al., 2021), and the role of human interpretations ("algorithmic brokers") once these systems are deployed in organizations (Waardenburg et al., 2022). Here, we also include work conducted in our lab on the use of no-code AI (Sundberg and Holmström, 2023), and as we engage more with generative AI, the importance of "prompt engineering" to facilitate innovation with large language models (Sundberg and Holmström, 2024b). A focal point in these papers is that they outline the necessity of having "humans-in-the-loop" during ML development and deployment. Thus, our teaching activities ensure that students not only acquire theoretical knowledge on the relation between humans and algorithms but that they achieve practical experience of what exactly it means to be in "the loop".

6. Plans to further develop the initiative

An AI for business course always needs to stay up to date with the latest developments in the field, but also balance the content to ensure it is appropriate for students from diverse backgrounds. While most of our work has been conducted within the specific course, we are now experiencing a range of synergy effects with other teaching and research initiatives. Plans to further develop the initiative include expanding the use of "no-code" AI platforms across more courses and disciplines and engaging in international collaborations to share best practices in teaching innovation and entrepreneurship. To further explore the use of these platforms in higher education, we have received a grant from the Swedish Research Council to conduct exploratory workshops with colleagues from European universities.

References

Geske, F., Hofmann, P., Lämmermann, L., Schlatt, V., & Urbach, N. (2021). Gateways to Artificial Intelligence: Developing a taxonomy for AI Service platforms. European Conference on Information Systems (ECIS).

Gröger, C. (2021). There is no AI without data. Communications of the ACM, 64(11), 98-108.

Humble, N., & Mozelius, P. (2022). The threat, hype, and promise of artificial intelligence in education. Discover Artificial Intelligence, 2(1), 1-13.

Kayhan, V. (2022). When to Use Machine Learning: A Course Assignment. Communications of the Association for Information Systems, vol 50, 122-142.

Lebovitz, S., Levina, N., & Lifshitz-Assaf, H. (2021). Is AI ground truth really true? The dangers of training and evaluating AI tools based on experts' know-what. MIS Quarterly, 45(3).

Lins, S., Pandl, K. D., Teigeler, H., Thiebes, S., Bayer, C., & Sunyaev, A. (2021). Artificial Intelligence as a Service, Business & Information Systems Engineering, 63(4), 441-456.

Luan, H., & Tsai, C. C. (2021). A review of using machine learning approaches for precision education. Educational Technology & Society, 24(1), 250-266.

Ma, Yizhi and Siau, Keng L. (2018) Artificial Intelligence Impacts on Higher Education. MWAIS 2018 Proceedings.

Merrill, M. D. (2012). First principles of instruction. John Wiley & Sons.

Schön, D. A. (2017). The reflective practitioner: How professionals think in action. Routledge.

Sundberg, L., & Holmström, J. (2022). Are AI Opportunities Discovered or Created? Investigating Data Resourcing Using a No-code AI Platform in an Educational Context. In Americas Conference on Information Systems.

Sundberg, L., & Holmström, J. (2023). Democratizing artificial intelligence: How no-code AI can leverage machine learning operations. Business Horizons, 66(6), 777-788.

Sundberg, L., & Holmström, J. (2024a). Teaching Tip: Using No-code AI to Teach Machine Learning in Higher Education. Journal of Information Systems Education, 35(1), 56-66.

Sundberg, L., & Holmström, J. (2024b). Innovating by prompting: How to facilitate innovation in the age of generative AI. Business Horizons.

Umeå University (2024). AI for business course curriculum, https://www.umu.se/en/education/syllabus/2in408/ accessed May 2024.

Van den Broek, E., Sergeeva, A., & Huysman, M. (2021). When the Machine Meets the Expert: An Ethnography of Developing AI for Hiring. MIS Quarterly, 45(3).

Waardenburg, L., Huysman, M., & Sergeeva, A. V. (2022). In the land of the blind, the one-eyed man is king: Knowledge brokerage in the age of learning algorithms. Organization Science, 33(1), 59-82.

Appendix A: Summarization of case narratives 2021-2023

Live case 1: WeldCorp (2021)
WeldCorp is a welding firm that was launched in Gothenburg, Sweden in 1994 by Kaj Kindvall, who serves as the CEO. The firm has grown steadily over the years, opening offices in Stockholm and Malmö in the early 2000s. By 2020, WeldCorp had further expanded its presence with additional facilities in northern Sweden. Kindvall's passion and focus on quality assurance have been important drivers of the company's growth. However, as WeldCorp has expanded, maintaining consistent service quality across multiple locations has become increasingly challenging. To address such challenges and sustain further growth, WeldCorp is now focusing on leveraging machine learning for quality assurance in its welding services. This strategic move aims to help the company

manage and maintain high-quality standards across all its operations despite the complexities introduced by rapid expansion, and new technologies.

Live case 2: RoboWeld (2022)
The firm "RoboWeld" is based in Umeå, Sweden, and focuses on the creation of agricultural machines. RoboWeld was founded in 1949 and began exporting products to international markets by the mid-1960s. The firm experienced rapid growth in the 1990s and early 2000s. By 2022 RoboWeld was one of the world's largest manufacturers in its industry. Now, the company seeks to integrate machine learning to enhance quality control and support long-term strategic goals. To achieve this, the firm is focusing on leveraging machine learning to detect "spatter" during the welding process. RoboWeld also aims to articulate an AI strategy that should outline important activities and their practical implementation, to ensure AI/ML technologies support long-term objectives.

Live case 3: InsureU (2023)
InsureU is a customer-centric insurance company in northern Sweden, with strong community ties. Under the leadership of its CEO, the company is navigating in a rapidly evolving insurance landscape, where digital-native competitors are challenging existing business models. Examples include data-driven decision-making and personalized services. This situation prompts InsureU to explore the potential of using AI/ML technologies for operational improvement and competitive advantage. One promising area identified for ML is the car damage case handling process, which is currently time-consuming and based on manual assessments. The CEO has identified a, partially labeled, dataset of damaged car images, as a potential resource for training a machine learning model to automate parts of the damage assessment process. The dataset includes labels such as "broken headlamp", "door scratch", and "bumper dent", among others.

Appendix B: Summarization of assignments 2021-2023

Assignment 2021:

Your assignment for this seminar is to help WeldCorp sustain its growth by leveraging machine learning. Specifically, your task is to analyze welding images (images of good and bad welding points) to develop a model – using the Peltarion AI platform – that can be useful for WeldCorp in a quality assurance context.

1. Describe and motivate your choices regarding the data processing, problem selection, and model training in the Peltarion platform.

2. Describe how you evaluated the predictions of your model. Are they accurate enough to use live for WeldCorp? Why / why not?

3. Discuss: What could be done by WeldCorp to improve the results of the model? How would they implement this type of solution in their business?

You will be presenting your results both in the form of a short paper, max ten pages, and orally at the final seminar. During the seminar, each group will get 30 minutes to present their results. You must also participate actively by answering questions and comments on the presentation. Your short paper should begin with a cover page on which you state the names of the group participants, the name of the course, and the semester. It is to be handed in at the beginning of the seminar.

The seminar will be graded with pass or fail. To get the grade pass you need to fulfill the following criteria:

- Present a logically coherent suggestion for WeldCorp, both in writing and orally during the seminar,
- Formulate your results and associated discussion in a grammatically correct way and with consistent use of concepts and terms.

Assignment 2022:

Your assignment for this seminar is to help RoboWeld create value by leveraging machine learning. Specifically, your task is to analyze welding images to detect "spatter". Spatter is an unwanted side-effect of the welding process and is constituted by small "drops" of metal near a welding joint. Here, your task is to develop a model – using the BigML platform – that can be useful for RoboWeld in a quality assurance context.

1. Describe and motivate your choices regarding data collecting/processing, problem selection, and model training in the AI platform.

2. Describe how you evaluated the predictions of your model. Are they accurate enough to use live for RoboWeld? Why / why not?

3. Discuss: What could be done by RoboWeld to improve the results of the model? How would they implement this type of solution in their business?

4. Articulate an AI strategy for RoboWeld with a particular focus on their value creation.

(+ a similar description of structure and criteria as above).

Assignment 2023:

Your *first* task is to:

1. Train a machine learning model in the BigML platform to differentiate between different types of car damage, and also add a class called "wrecked", signaling that the car is not to be repaired but ready for the scrap yard.
A) Describe the considerations you made during the ML workflow (data collection/labeling/model training and evaluation).
B) How can your model be used at InsureU, and does it perform well enough for this purpose? Why / why not?

Your *second* task is to:

2. Formulate a basis for building a so-called "GPT" in ChatGPT4, to make it able to classify car damage based on images sent in by a customer. To do this, you need to engage with the art of "prompting" to set the proper tone and give the GPT instructions on how to react when a customer sends an image of a damaged car:

A) You want to use a LLM to interact with customers when they are reporting car damage (= they submit an image of their damaged car). Similar to the model trained during step 1, the GPT should be able to identify the type of damage and if the car should be scrapped. Formulate a prompt that describes the behavior of the GPT, and criteria for its assessment of an image. Make sure to describe the logic and sources used during this step.

B) In addition to communicating with customers, you want the GPT to format and send the report of the damaged car in a machine-readable format for further processing by InsureU's systems. Add this to the instructions for the GPT.

(+ a similar description of structure and criteria as above).

Author biographies

Leif Sundberg is an associate professor at the Department of Informatics, Umeå University. Sundberg's research interests involve digital government, the use of no-code artificial intelligence, and risk society studies. Sundberg has a broad teaching experience in engineering management and information systems. He has published his work in journals such as The Journal of Strategic Information Systems, Business Horizons, and Journal of Information Systems Education.

Jonny Holmström is a professor of Information Systems at Umeå University and director and co-founder of the Swedish Center for Digital Innovation. His research interests are digital innovation, digital transformation, and digital entrepreneurship. He is serving on the editorial boards of CAIS, EJIS, Information and Organization, and JAIS. His work has appeared in journals such as European Journal of Information Systems, Information and Organization, Information Systems Journal, Journal of the AIS, Journal of Information Technology, Journal of Strategic Information Systems, and MIS Quarterly.

www.ingramcontent.com/pod-product-compliance
Lightning Source LLC
Chambersburg PA
CBHW072159160426
43197CB00012B/2449